The Complete Idiot's Word for Windows Reference Card

(You Mean I ... ...riting This Book, and ... ... to Read It?)

Scrolling Through a Document with the Keyboard

To move . . .	Press . . .
Up or down one line	Up or down arrow key
Left or right one character	Left or right arrow key
One word left or right	Ctrl and either the left or right arrow key
Up or down one paragraph	Ctrl and either the up or down arrow key
Up or down one screen	Page Up or Page Down
Top of the screen	Ctrl+Page Up
Bottom of the screen	Ctrl+Page Down
Beginning of the line	Home
End of the line	End
Beginning of document	Ctrl+Home
End of document	Ctrl+End
Toggle between two panes	F6
Move to the next cell in a table	Tab
Move to a previous cell in a table	Shift+Tab

Selecting Text with the Mouse

To select this . . .	Do this . . .
Word	Double-click on word.
Sentence	Press Ctrl and click on sentence.
Line	Click in front of the line.
Multiple lines	Drag in the selection bar next to the lines.
Paragraph	Double-click in front of paragraph.
Column	Click at top of column.
Row	Click in front of row.
Whole document	Press Ctrl and click in selection bar.

Get Out Your Tools!

Icon		Function
	New	Opens a new document.
	Open	Opens an existing document.
	Save	Saves the document you're working on.
	Cut	Removes text and stores it for placement elsewhere.
	Copy	Copies text for placement elsewhere.
	Paste	Inserts stored text at current location.
	Undo	Undoes the last action or command.
	Numbered List	Changes text to numbered list style.
	Bulleted List	Changes text to bulleted list style.
	Unindent	Moves the left margin back to the previous tab stop.
	Indent	Moves the left margin forward to the next tab stop.
	Table	Changes text to table style.
	Text Columns	Changes text to newspaper-style columns.
	Frame	Inserts a frame for handling text, graphics, and tables.
	Draw	Starts Microsoft Draw.
	Graph	Starts Microsoft Graph.
	Envelope	Prints an envelope.
	Spelling	Checks the current document for spelling errors.
	Print	Prints the current document.
	Zoom Whole Page	Allows you to view the entire current page on the screen.
	Zoom 100 Percent	Allows you to view the document at its normal size.
	Zoom Page Width	Allows you to view the document so its full width is displayed.

alpha books

Tie a Yellow Ribbon 'Round the Ol' Word Screen

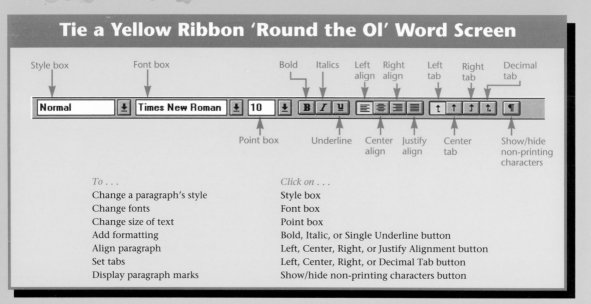

To . . .	Click on . . .
Change a paragraph's style	Style box
Change fonts	Font box
Change size of text	Point box
Add formatting	Bold, Italic, or Single Underline button
Align paragraph	Left, Center, Right, or Justify Alignment button
Set tabs	Left, Center, Right, or Decimal Tab button
Display paragraph marks	Show/hide non-printing characters button

The Anatomy of a Ruler

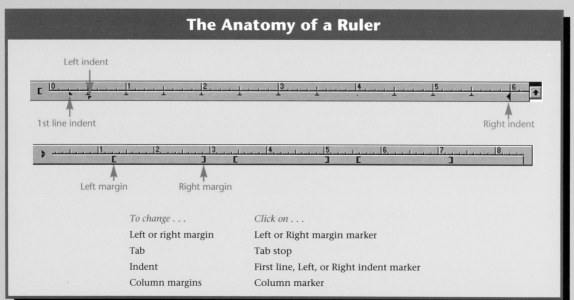

To change . . .	Click on . . .
Left or right margin	Left or Right margin marker
Tab	Tab stop
Indent	First line, Left, or Right indent marker
Column margins	Column marker

Formatting Text with the Keyboard

To change characters to . . .	Press this key combination:
Bold	Ctrl+B
Italic	Ctrl+I
Single Underline	Ctrl+U
Word Underline	Ctrl+W
Double Underline	Ctrl+D
Small Caps	Ctrl+K
All Caps	Ctrl+A
Hidden	Ctrl+H
Superscript	Ctrl+Shift+Plus Sign

Formatting Paragraphs with the Keyboard

To change paragraphs to this . . .	Press this key combination:
Left-aligned text	Ctrl+L
Right-aligned text	Ctrl+R
Centered text	Ctrl+E
Justified text	Ctrl+J
Normal style	Alt+Shift+5 (on numeric keypad)
Change styles	Ctrl+S
Remove manual formatting	Ctrl+Q

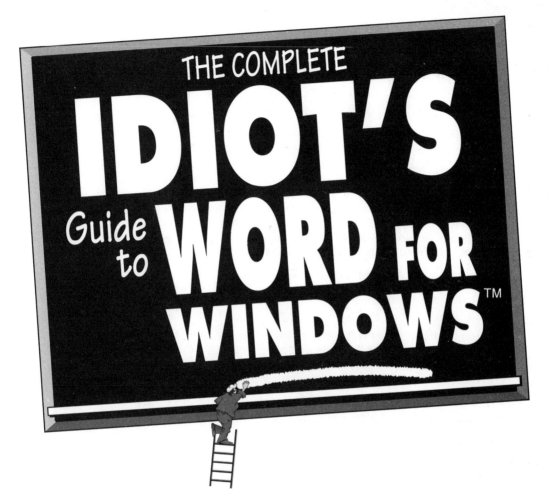

THE COMPLETE
IDIOT'S
Guide to WORD FOR WINDOWS™

by Jennifer Flynn

alpha
books

A Division of Prentice Hall Computer Publishing
11711 North College Avenue, Carmel, Indiana 46032 USA

To my sister Beth, a kind-hearted soul with a never-ending amount of patience (that I seem to test the limits of constantly). I'm lucky to have her as a sister and a best friend.

©1993 Alpha Books

International Standard Book Number: 1-56761-174-5
Library of Congress Catalog Card Number: 93-70015

96 95 94 93   8 7 6 5 4 3 2

Interpretation of the printing code: the rightmost number of the first series of numbers is the year of the book's printing; the rightmost number of the second series of numbers is the number of the book's printing. For example, a printing code of 93-1 shows that the first printing of the book occurred in 1993.

Screen reproductions in this book were created by means of the Collage Plus program from Inner Media, Inc., Hollis, NH.

Printed in the United States of America

Publisher
Marie Butler-Knight

Associate Publisher
Lisa A. Bucki

Managing Editor
Elizabeth Keaffaber

Acquisitions Manager
Stephen R. Poland

Development Editor
Faithe Wempen

Production Editor
Annalise N. Di Paolo

Copy Editor
Audra Gable

Cover Designer
Scott Cook

Designer
Amy Peppler-Adams

Illustrator
Steve Vanderbosch

Indexer
Jeanne Clark

Production Team
*Diana Bigham, Scott Cook, Tim Cox, Mark Enochs, Tom Loveman,
Roger Morgan, Joe Ramon, Carrie Roth, Greg Simsic, Mary Beth Wakefield*

*Special thanks to C. Herbert Feltner for ensuring the
technical accuracy of this book.*

Contents at a Glance

Contents

13 Now You're Ready for the Big Time: Formatting a Document   133

14 Setting Your Own Style   143

15 Picking Up the Tab for the Whole Table   153

Introduction

You're not an idiot, but if Word for Windows makes you feel like one, you need a book that can help. What you *don't* need is a book that assumes you are (or want to become) a Word wizard. You don't need someone to tell you that Word for Windows is one of the most complex word processors around. (You've already learned that the hard way.) You're a busy person with a real life, and you're just trying to get a stupid letter, memo, or report, written, spell-checked, and printed.

Why Do You Need This Book?

With so many computer books on the market, why do you need this one? Well, first off, this book won't assume that you know anything at all about how to use Word for Windows, or Windows itself for that matter.

This book doesn't assume that you want (or have the time) to learn everything there is to know about Word for Windows. The most common tasks are broken down into easy-to-read chapters that you can finish in a short time. Simply open the book when you have a question or a problem, read what you need to, and get back to your life.

How Do I Use This Book?

For starters, don't actually *read* this book (at least not the whole thing). When you need a quick answer, use the Table of Contents or the Index to find the right section. Each section is self-contained, with exactly what you need to know to solve your problem or to answer your question.

If you're supposed to press a particular key, you'll know it because that key will appear in bold, as in

Press **Enter** to continue.

Sometimes you'll be asked to press two keys at the same time. This is called a *key combination*. Key combinations appear in this book with a plus sign between them. The plus means that you should hold the first key down while you press the second key listed. For example:

Press **Alt+F** to open the File menu.

In this case, you should hold the **Alt** key down while you press the letter **F**, and then something will happen. Alt is a pretty popular key; it's used practically with all the letters on the keyboard to do one thing or another (more on this later). The bold letter F that you see in the word **File** is there to remind you that this time, you should press the letter F with the Alt key.

There are some special boxed notes in this book that will help you learn just what you need:

> ## By the Way . . .
> Special hints from yours truly.

> ## Put It to Work
> Safe ways to practice what you learn.

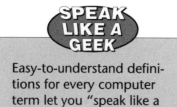

Easy-to-understand definitions for every computer term let you "speak like a geek."

Skip this background fodder (technical twaddle) unless you're truly interested.

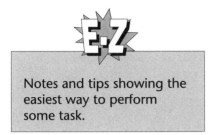

Notes and tips showing the easiest way to perform some task.

Help when things go wrong.

Make sure to watch for the special "What's Wrong with This Picture?" sections; they highlight simple exercises that test what you've learned.

Acknowledgments

Thanks to everyone at Alpha Books that helped with this book. It's nice to be part of such a great team.

Very special thanks to Scott (my Gibraltar) for supplying me with love, patience, and tons of good suggestions during the writing of this book.

Trademarks

All terms mentioned in this book that are known to be trademarks or service marks are listed below. In addition, terms suspected of being trademarks or service marks have been appropriately capitalized. Alpha Books cannot attest to the accuracy of this information. Use of a term in this book should not be regarded as affecting the validity of any trademark or service mark.

CorelDRAW! is a registered trademark of Corel Systems Corporation.

DrawPerfect is a registered trademark of WordPerfect Corporation.

Lotus 1-2-3 is a registered trademark of Lotus Development.

Microsoft Excel, Word for Windows, Microsoft Graph, Microsoft Windows, Microsoft Word are registered trademarks of Microsoft Corporation.

PageMaker is a registered trademark of Aldus Corporation.

PC Paintbrush is a registered trademark of ZSoft Corporation.

Quattro Pro is a registered trademark of Borland International, Inc.

Ventura Publisher is a registered trademark of Ventura Software, Inc.

Part I
Dad Does
Word Processing

My dad used to work at home a lot, and one day my brother Mike decided that Dad needed a computer, so he bought him one. After getting him started with a few basics ("Here's the keyboard; just type"), Mike left him alone. Later, Dad showed me a letter he'd just printed: two paragraphs followed by four blank pages. Dad was very puzzled by this, so he asked, "Do you think it needs a new ribbon?" I could tell that Mike had left out some of the essentials.

That's the problem with most computer books today; they assume you know something, and they end up leaving out the essentials. In this section, you'll learn all those things Mike should have told my dad about using a word processor (including the fact that you shouldn't lean the manual against the Enter key or you'll end up producing four blank pages).

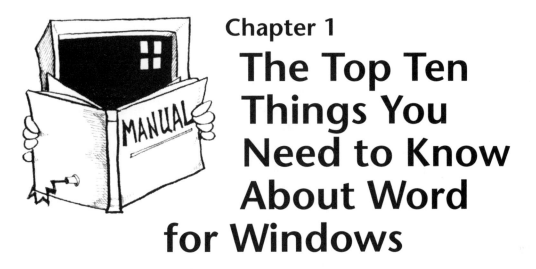

Chapter 1

The Top Ten Things You Need to Know About Word for Windows

Just like those other "notes" you used to buy in high school to avoid actually reading books, here's a Jennifer's Notes version of the amazing facts you'll find within these pages. If you read nothing else in this book, for gosh sakes, read this!

1. **Word for Windows is a Windows program,** so you must know something about Windows in order to use it. If you're a stranger to Windows, read Chapter 3, and I'll introduce the two of you.

2. **Don't press Enter at the end of each line—only at the end of a paragraph.** If you're accustomed to using a typewriter, you're also used to returning the carriage to the left margin at the end of every line. Word processors are different; when you press Enter, you create a new paragraph. So how do you get to the next line if you don't press Enter? Well, as you type, words *wrap* between the left and right margins automatically. If you add or delete text in a paragraph, the existing text adjusts itself to fit the margins. Chapter 6 explains the ins and outs of typing text.

3. **Don't use the Spacebar to center text.** If you want your heading to be centered, don't use the Spacebar to move to the starting position. Instead, select center alignment (which centers any amount of text between the left and right margins). In Chapter 12, you'll learn how to set up centered, right-aligned, or left-aligned text.

4. **Save your work often.** Even a momentary power outage can make a simply horrible day even worse. When you turn off your computer, everything you're working on is erased from the computer's memory—so *save, save, save* it onto a disk! Better yet, make Word for Windows save your documents at timed intervals, so you won't ever be caught with your computer down. In Chapter 9, you'll learn how to save your documents.

5. **Word for Windows is a very versatile fellow.** You can issue commands (such as saving your document) to Word for Windows in a number of ways: by selecting them off a menu (a list), by clicking on a picture that represents the action you want to take (an icon), or by pressing several keys at the same time. You'll learn how to take command of Word for Windows in Chapter 4.

6. **When you want to change how text looks, select it!** Select the text you want, then click on a button or select a menu command to change it. For example, you can select a heading by moving to the beginning of the text, pressing and holding the left mouse button, and moving to the end of the text to highlight it. Once the heading is selected, you can choose commands to make the heading larger, bold, and underlined. In Chapter 6, you'll learn how to select text.

7. **If you're used to WordPerfect, Word lets you ease in slowly.** Word for Windows contains support for all the WordPerfect keyboard shortcuts (such as Shift+F10 to retrieve a document). Word for Windows also contains WordPerfect Help and special tutorials to get you up and running in Word. Turn to Chapter 5 for more help in moving from WordPerfect to Word for Windows.

8. **What you see isn't always what you get.** The default viewing mode for Word for Windows is Normal. In Normal mode, you will not see pictures, graphs, and columns as they will appear when printed. Use Print Preview mode to view a document just before printing. Chapter 7 describes all the ways you can look at your document.

9. **Word for Windows lets you use all your Windows programs together.** Word for Windows can import part of a spreadsheet from any Windows program, such as Excel or Lotus for Windows. It can even create a link between your document and the imported item's native program so that changes made to the imported item are automatically reflected in your document. In Chapter 21, you'll learn how to import data and pictures from other programs.

10. **You can perform all of your editing tasks faster and easier with a mouse than with the keyboard.** Just about any type of task, such as changing the look of text or saving or printing a document, can be done faster and easier with a mouse. With the Toolbar and Ribbon, you click on a button to make changes or perform some task. You say you don't know how to use a mouse? Don't worry—you'll learn all about it in Chapter 3.

Okay, so I lied. But I just couldn't resist adding something about one of the most powerful features of Word.

11. **Word for Windows lets you create your own style.** The style of a paragraph controls how it should look—its margins, alignment (such as centered), indentations, and so on. For example, you can create a Heading style that makes your headings bold and centered. By changing one of the style's settings, you change all paragraphs of that style in one simple step. For example, if you changed the Heading style to include underline, then all of the headings within your document would change to bold, centered, and underlined. Chapter 14 gives you the lowdown on styles— how to create them and how to use them.

This page unintentionally left blank.

Chapter 2
A Kinder, Gentler Introduction to Word Processing

In This Chapter

- ☞ What is a word processor?
- ☞ Why learning to use a word processor is worth the time
- ☞ Things you can do with a word processor
- ☞ What is desktop publishing?

The Stone Age: Using a Typewriter to Record Thought

Back in the Stone Age of typewriters and correction fluid, the simple act of typing a letter or a memo was often brought to a halt by the ever-present red pen. Ogg would groan as his boss filled the pages with red lines, deletion marks, and new text. Ogg would then return crestfallen to his desk and retype the entire 10-page report. Poor Ogg—if only he'd had a *word processor*.

What Makes a Word Processor So Great?

Admittedly, learning to use a word processor takes a bit more time than learning to use a typewriter, but look at the advantages: no more correction fluid on your fingers, no more sticky letter keys to unjam, no more platen grease smearing the sides of an important paper. (I, for one, do not miss my typewriter.) Ogg could have made all of his boss's changes and still been home in time for a hot bowl of woolly-mammoth stew—but no! Instead of chucking his typewriter into the nearest tar pit, Ogg retyped the entire report. With a word processor, Ogg easily could have made all these changes (and more):

☛ Inserting text into existing paragraphs, and having everything move down and stay within the margins.

☛ Deleting text with the same ease as inserting new text—everything would just "self-adjust" between the margins.

☛ Checking the report for spelling errors before printing it out.

☛ Easily centering his title and adding bold lettering to make it stand out.

☛ Adding a big chart that made the report so nice-looking that his boss got a promotion, and Ogg got parking privileges for his dinosaur.

☛ Printing out an extra copy of the report for his own files, instead of spending half the Stone Age waiting at the copier.

☛ Adjusting the report for next month by changing some figures and replacing the word "March" with "April" throughout the report.

Without a word processor, Ogg probably spent the rest of his life retyping the same report—but not you! Armed with your Word for Windows program and this nifty book, you'll learn how to do all these things and more.

A Day in the Life of a Word Processor

As you create your document in Word for Windows, you'll follow a basic pattern:

Open an existing document, or create a new one. You start your work session by typing text into a new document, or by editing an existing one. You'll learn about working with documents in Chapter 8.

Type in some text. This part is easy; just type! Okay, there are some things you should know before you start typing, and you'll learn them in this chapter and in Chapter 6.

Read what you've written and make changes. At this stage, you're copying or moving text from one place to another. You may even delete some text or insert new text to clarify a point. The process of making changes to existing text is called *editing*. You'll learn some easy editing techniques in Chapter 6.

Add pizzazz. Changing the way characters look (such as adding bold or making characters bigger) is called *formatting*. You'll learn how to format text in Chapter 11.

Spell check your document. Word comes with a spell checker that checks your words. You can also use the Word grammar checker to look for errors in context. Of course, nothing can replace the actual process of re-reading your text for sense, but these powerful tools help ensure that your documents look professional. You'll learn more about them in Chapter 16.

Save your document. Once you're sure you have a document that you like, you should save it. Actually, it's best to save a document often during the editing phase so you can't lose any changes. You'll learn how to save your document in Chapter 9.

View your document before you print it. Word gives you lots of ways to view your text both as you are working and right before you print your document. You'll learn all you need to know about viewing a document in Chapter 7.

Print your document. Nothing is better than holding the finished product in your own hands. You'll learn how to print your documents in Chapter 10.

Oggs and Ends of Using a Word Processor

Before you begin to use a word processor, you need to understand a few things:

The thing that you create with a word processor is called a document. Document is just a hoity-toity word for something like a memo, a letter, or a report. If you ask a PC guru for help, make sure you throw it in (if you can do an English accent, it's even better): "Pardon me, but I think I'm having trouble with this *document*."

The cursor marks the place where text will be inserted. The *cursor* is a horizontal line that acts like the tip of a pencil; anything you type appears at the cursor. You'll learn more about the cursor as we go on. To be real cool, call the cursor by its nickname: *insertion point.*

What you see isn't necessarily what you get. The right-hand margin that you see on your screen may not be the right-hand margin of your document. Word for Windows has several ways you can view your document on-screen; in one mode, the text is large and comfortable to work with, but you may not see the right-hand margin of your document when you work in that mode. You'll learn more about viewing modes in Chapter 7.

A dotted line marks the end of a page. Just cross over the dotted line when you see it; a dotted line tells Word for Windows where one page ends and another begins. If you add text above a dotted line, the excess text at the bottom of that page will flow onto the next page automatically.

Formatting describes the way something looks. Character *formatting* describes how a character looks (for example, is it **bold** or *italic?*). Paragraph formatting describes the alignment of a paragraph (for example, is it centered?). To save time, you can save the formatting of a paragraph as a *style,* and reapply that same formatting to many paragraphs with a few keystrokes.

Microsoft Word - \PROJECTS\WW\FIGS\MARKET.DOC

File　Edit　View　Insert　Format　Tools　Table　Window　Help

Normal　　Arial　　10　　B I U

high priority so as to guarantee our dominance against those who might come after.

• *Customer Satisfaction:* ──────────── **Text is format-ted in italic.**

Our marketing research shows that a large percentage of people who use glamour services are women, and that they come to be pampered. Care must be taken to ensure a comfortable, open environment in which our customer will feel free to be a star.

Change your view to see text near the right margin.

A wide selection of clothes will be available to meet all the customers needs, along with professional hair stylists, manicurists (hands may not show in all photos, but the feeling of glamour and pampering is what we are going for here.,) along with facial consultants, set designers, and photo consultants.

End of page

Ample time must be given for a complete session. Under no circumstances is the customer feel rushed.

Market Share Projections

Extensive market research has shown that glamour photography is one of the hottest growth areas today. With fair pricing, comfortable surroundings, and professional staff, our glamour studios will dominate the

Pg 1　Sec 1　1/2　At 8.1"　Ln 34　Col 1　100%　NUM

Cursor or insertion point　　Your document

The ins and outs and odds and ends of using a word processor.

So What's All This Fuss About Desktop Publishing?

"High-end" (in other words, expensive) word processors, such as Word for Windows, give you a lot of bang for your buck by including tons of features you'll probably never use. It's not that the people at Microsoft want to confuse you by including too much stuff; it's just that when you need to do something special with a piece of paper, they want you to be able to do it with Word for Windows, so you don't go off and try some other product. One of the special things you may do someday is *desktop publishing*.

Desktop publishing The process of combining text and graphics on the same page or manipulating the text and graphics on-screen. Desktop publishing is used to create newsletters, brochures, flyers, resumes, and business cards.

Graphic

Add a border or some shading to add pizzazz!

Text formatted as columns

When you take a picture and slap it on a page with text, you're a desktop publisher!

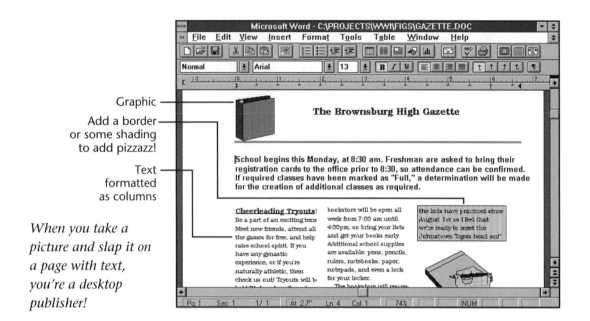

Although you can do a few of the more popular desktop publishing chores (typing text in columns, placing graphics anywhere on a page, or adding borders and shading to emphasize certain words) in Word for Windows, if you want to do anything fancy, you should invest in a real desktop publishing program, such as PageMaker or Ventura Publisher. If you just can't wait to start your desktop publishing career, skip ahead to Chapters 20 and 21 for instructions on how to manipulate text and graphics in Word.

The Least You Need to Know

It's a kinder, gentler world out there thanks to word processors. Never again will you be faced with a dried-up bottle of White-out. And what's more, a word processor is so much faster than a typewriter when you need to

- ☞ Insert and delete text from an existing document.

- ☞ Check for spelling and grammatical errors.

- ☞ Punch up your prose with bold, underline, and italic.

- ☞ Add pizzazz to your documents with charts and graphics.

- ☞ Print extra copies of your documents.

Chapter 3
For Those of Us Who Don't Do Windows

In This Chapter

- ☞ How to get Windows started
- ☞ How to use a mouse
- ☞ The parts of a Windows window
- ☞ Adjusting windows to fit the way you want to work
- ☞ Closing windows
- ☞ Sizing a window so it's "just right"
- ☞ Exiting the Windows program

When I was first learning to use Windows, I felt overwhelmed. I'd never really used a mouse before, and all those boxes on my screen made me feel like a moving company. The only thought that kept me going was that (for the most part) I'd never see that ol' DOS prompt again. Also, I knew that once I learned the basics of using the mouse and manipulating windows, I'd know most of what I needed to use *all my Windows programs*.

What you'll learn in this chapter is the basic stuff you'll use every day, in every Windows program—including Word for Windows.

A Logical Place to Start

I am occasionally hit by bouts of logic, and during a recent episode, it occurred to me that before I show you how to use Windows, I should show you how to start it. It's relatively easy:

Turn on your computer. Look for a switch on the front, back, or right-hand side of that big box thing. You may also have to turn on your *monitor* (it looks like a TV, but it gets lousy reception).

After you turn on your computer, Windows may start all by itself. If it does, pass Go and skip on down to the next section.

If you get a menu listing Windows as one of the options, press the number in front of your selection, then press **Enter**.

If instead you get a rather unassuming DOS prompt that resembles C> or C:\>, type

      WIN

and press **Enter**.

Minimize button

Program Manager window

Windows desktop

Word for Windows program group

Active programs minimized to icons

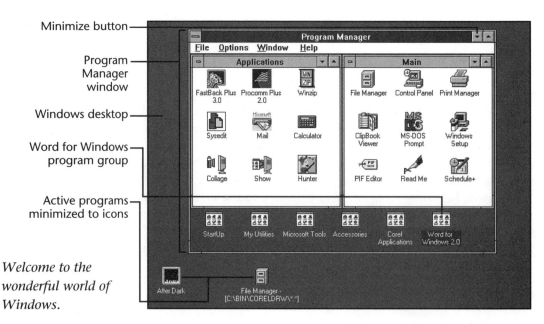

Welcome to the wonderful world of Windows.

Don't panic if your screen doesn't look exactly like mine; that's the point of Windows—you can customize it to work the way you do. When you start Windows, the main program, Program Manager, is usually open and ready to go. *Program Manager* helps you switch between programs and customize the way your programs work with Windows.

Making Friends with a Mouse

Using Windows (and Windows programs like Word for Windows) without a mouse is like trying to pull something out of the oven without mitts. It can be done, but why take the chance of getting burned? So play it smart; get a *mouse!*

To get to know your mouse quickly, here are some easy tips:

Mouse   A device attached to your computer that controls a pointer on your screen. To move the pointer to the left, move the mouse to the left. To move the pointer to the right, move the mouse to the right, and so on.

Mouse pad   A small square of plastic or foam that the mouse rests on. A mouse pad provides better traction than your desktop, and keeps the mouse away from dust and other goop on your desk.

Point   To move the mouse pointer so that it is on top of a specific object on-screen.

The proper way to hold your furless friend.

☞ Place the mouse in the middle of the *mouse pad,* with its cord extending away from you.

If you use Windows on a portable computer, such as a laptop, you may have a "dead mouse"—but don't set any rat traps just yet! You don't move this kind of mouse, which is why it's nicknamed a "dead mouse." (Its real name is *trackball*.) A trackball has its roller ball on top, and you move the mouse pointer by moving the roller ball with your thumb.

Click   To click with the mouse, press and release the mouse button once.

Double-click   To double-click with the mouse, press and release the mouse button twice quickly.

Drag   To drag with the mouse, first move the pointer to the starting position. Now press and hold the left mouse button. Move (drag) the pointer to the ending position, and then release the mouse button.

☞ Rest your hand on the mouse, with your palm at its base. Grip the mouse with your thumb and ring finger. When curled, your fingers should rest lightly on the buttons at the top of the mouse. Rest your index finger on the left mouse button and your middle finger on the right button. (If your mouse has a middle button, ignore it.)

☞ Move the little guy around. Don't be surprised if this feels a bit funny—remember what it felt like to hold a pencil for the first time? To me, it felt like I was holding a broomstick between my fingers. The pencil kept slipping out of my hands, and I just couldn't get the hang of it. But you'll get used to your furless friend in no time.

☞ Practice moving the mouse on the mouse pad, to make the on-screen pointer point to different boxes and windows. (I know what your mother always told you, but in this case, it's polite to point.) If you move the mouse slowly, the pointer will move slowly, and about the same distance. If you move the mouse fast, the pointer steps on the gas and moves a greater distance on-screen.

☞ If you run out of mouse pad but you need to move further on the screen, just pick that critter up and place it back in the middle of the pad. When you lift the mouse, the pointer doesn't move; it's the roller on the bottom that moves it.

Right on the (Left) Button!

After you've pointed at something on-screen with the pointer, either click or double-click with the left mouse button (unless specifically told to use

the right) to perform an action. Some actions require that you *drag* the mouse (no, not along the floor).

As a general rule of thumb, you click on things to highlight or choose them, double-click to activate them, and drag to select them.

By the Way . . .

I move my mouse by using short strokes: I move it a little, pick it up (just barely), place it back in the middle of the pad, and move it again. It's like those cars that kids wind up by pushing them on the floor: you just keep moving the mouse in short strokes, over the same small spot on the mouse pad. This way, you never lose control of the mouse, and it always stays in the middle of the mouse pad. (I call this technique "rowing," and it constitutes a large part of my daily exercise program.)

Put It to Work

Mousing Around

Point to the Program Manager's Minimize button. Move the mouse pointer so that it rests on top of the downward pointing arrow. (Look back at the first figure in this chapter if you need help.)

Click on the Minimize button. Press the left mouse button once while pointing with the mouse to the downward pointing arrow. Clicking on the Minimize button chooses it, and the Program Manager becomes an icon at the bottom of the screen.

Point to the Program Manager icon. Move the mouse pointer so that it rests on top of the Program Manager icon.

Double-click on the Program Manager icon to open it. Press the left mouse button two times quickly while pointing to the Program Manager icon. Double-clicking on the icon activates the Program Manager, and it reopens its window.

Now that you know how to use a mouse, you're ready to move on to something with a lot more buttons: the keyboard.

Playing with a Full Keyboard

Microsoft devised Windows and Word for Windows to work more easily with a mouse or trackball than with a keyboard. However, there are some special key combinations that, although they force your hands into painful positions, will allow you to perform a common task without using a mouse. Pressing multiple keys at the same time (such as Ctrl+Shift+F12, a key combination that tells Word to print your document) will make you great at creating shadow puppets. But personally it makes my hands ache, so I'm going to speak to you throughout this book as though you own a mouse. Windows without a mouse is about as pointless as lasagna without the pasta.

> ### By the Way . . .
> If you're allergic to mice, or if you are switching from a keyboard-intense word processor, such as WordPerfect, you may prefer using the keyboard over using a mouse. So in Chapter 4, I'll show you how to use the keyboard to select commands. But you should still make an effort to learn to use the mouse for moving and copying text; it's the fastest and easiest way!

Using a mouse in a word processor doesn't mean that you'll never use the keyboard, so here goes. If you've ever used a typewriter, you'll notice that the computer keyboard is similar, but different. Don't let all those keys intimidate you—the keyboard is easy to use when you learn the functions of the keys.

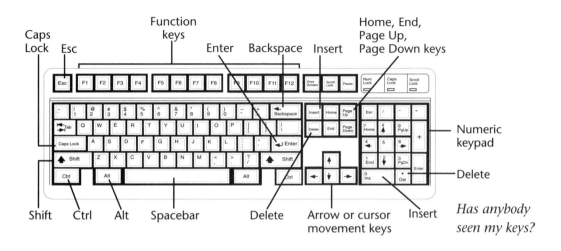

Here are the functions of some of the keys that are not so obvious:

Enter   In Word for Windows, you press the Enter key at the end of a paragraph (any grouping of words that should be treated as a unit). This includes normal paragraphs as well as single-line paragraphs, such as chapter titles, section headings, and captions for charts or other figures.

By the Way . . .

The Enter key is something that computer manufacturers like to hide. The Enter key is often marked by a bent arrow pointing to the left and sometimes by the word Return.

Esc   Called the Escape key, Esc is used to cancel commands or to back out of an operation in Word.

Function keys   These keys are sometimes called the F keys because they all begin with an F. You'll find them either at the top or on the left-hand side of the keyboard. Each program assigns its own special meanings to them. For example, in Word for Windows, F1 means Help, and F2 means Move.

Shift   Used just like a typewriter to type capital letters and special characters, such as #$%?>. In some programs, you can use the Shift key with other keys to issue commands with the keyboard. For example, in Word for Windows, Shift+F2 means Copy.

Alt and Ctrl   The Alt and Ctrl keys are used like the Shift key; press them with another key to issue commands with the keyboard. For example, in Word for Windows, Ctrl+F2 increases the size of the selected text.

Caps Lock   This locks in capital letters. But unlike a typewriter, you will not get ! when you press the 1 key (even with the Caps Lock on). To get ! when the Caps Lock is on, you must still press the Shift key and 1 at the same time—likewise with @, #, and other special characters.

Backspace   Press this key to erase the letter or number to the left of the cursor. Use the Backspace key to erase all or part of a paragraph.

Arrow or cursor movement keys   Hmmm Kemosabe, the cursor go that way. (These keys will make the cursor move in the direction of the arrow.)

Spacebar   Use the Spacebar to insert a space between words and at the end of sentences. Don't be a space cadet and use the Spacebar to move the cursor—use the arrow keys or the mouse instead.

Insert (Ins)   If Insert is on (which is the default in Word for Windows), what you type is inserted between characters beginning at the current cursor position. Press this key to switch to Overtype mode, and what you type will replace existing characters.

Delete (Del)   Deletes the character to the right of the cursor.

Home, End, Page Up, Page Down keys   Home moves the cursor to the beginning of a line; End moves the cursor to the end of a line; Page Down displays the next screen of text; and Page Up displays the previous screen.

Windows You Don't Look Through

The basic component of Windows is (not surprisingly) windows. Windows are boxes on your screen that you can open, close, move, resize, and otherwise manipulate to your heart's content: you have total control of what's displayed on your screen. Let's open a window so we have something to look at:

Point to the Word for Windows program group icon. A program group is a special window that's used to group several applications together. For example, in the Word for Windows program group, you find two program icons: Microsoft Word and Word Setup. A program group *icon* is simply a program group that's been minimized (reduced to an icon when you click on its Minimize button).

Double-click on the program group icon to open the program group. Press the mouse button two times in quick succession while pointing to the Word for Windows program group icon.

Maximize the Word for Windows program group. Click on the **Maximize** button. The Word for Windows program group will grow to fill the Program Manager window; it will not fill the screen unless the Program Manager itself is maximized.

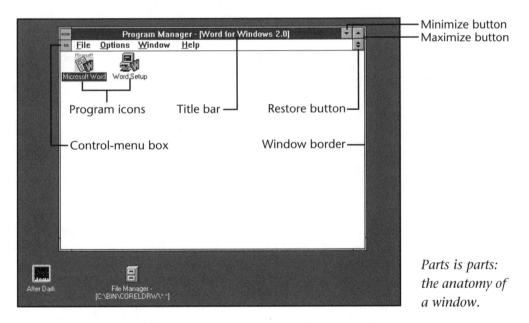

Parts is parts: the anatomy of a window.

Now that the window is open, let's look at its parts:

Title bar   This displays the title for the window.

Control-menu box   Click here to display a menu with commands for resizing, closing, and moving windows.

Minimize button   Click here to reduce the window to an icon at the bottom of your screen.

Maximize button   Click here to increase the window to fill your screen.

Restore button   Click here to restore the window to its previous size.

In Windows, you can run multiple programs at the same time. For example, you can run a *spreadsheet program* and Word for Windows and jump between the two whenever you wish. Each program you start has its own window, and that window will take up all or part of the screen, depending on how you size it. By manipulating your windows, you can see several programs at one time, and fly between them with the greatest of ease.

By the Way . . .

Why is the ability to run multiple programs such a big deal? With two programs running at the same time, it's easy to exchange data from one to the other. For example, you could compute the department budget in a spreadsheet program and then copy that data into your department report within Word for Windows.

Sizing Up Windows

Changing the size of a window is easy. You can restore the Word for Windows program group window to the size it was before you maximized it. Click on the **Restore** button now (the double-headed arrow) to restore the window.

You can maximize the window again by clicking on the **Maximize** button (the upward pointing arrow). Go ahead and do that now.

If you click on the Restore button again, the window will be returned to its former petite self. Click on the **Restore** button and watch that weight come off!

You can minimize a window (reduce it to an icon at the bottom of the Program Manager window) by clicking on the Minimize button. Minimize the Word for Windows program group now by clicking on the **Minimize** button (the downward pointing arrow).

You can open a minimized window by double-clicking on the window's icon. Go ahead and double-click—it'll make you feel good!

Goldilocks Does Windows

If a window is too big when it's maximized, and too small when it's minimized, how do you resize a window so it's *just right?* You drag it!

Let's practice on our Word for Windows program group window. To resize a window, move the pointer very slowly to the window's edge. (The mouse pointer will turn into a double-headed arrow.) Now press the left mouse button (click) and *hold it down*. While you're holding the mouse button down, drag the edge outward to make the window bigger, or inward to make it smaller. You'll see a ghostly image of the window edge as you drag. As long as you hold the mouse button down, you can play with the window's size as long as you want. When you've got the window "just right," release the mouse button.

When you minimize a window, sometimes it plays hide-and-seek behind other open windows. If you can't find the Word for Windows program group after minimizing it, open the **W**indow menu by clicking on it or by pressing **Alt+W**. When the menu is open, select the Word for Windows program group from the list by clicking on it or pressing its number.

If a window is maximized so that it fills your screen, you won't be able to resize it manually, because it won't have a border. (What a drag!) Instead, click on the **Restore** button to restore the window to its previous size, and then manually resize it if necessary.

A window cannot be bigger than the Program Manager window. If you look back at the last figure, you'll see that the Program Manager window does not fill my screen. (That gray background you see is the Windows desktop, and the Program Manager sits on top of it.) However, you can maximize your Program Manager window so it fills the screen; then any window that's maximized within it will also fill the screen.

Moving Day

Before I can start work, everything has to be in its proper place on my desk. I put my coffee cup to the left of my computer, the mouse pad to the right, and books and other reference items that I plan on tripping over all day are on the floor.

When you work in Windows, you can move your windows around until you get everything in "its proper place." To move a window, you drag it by its title bar.

Let's practice on our Word for Windows program group window. Point at the title bar at the top of the window. Then press the left mouse button (click) and *hold it down*. While you're holding the mouse button down, drag the title bar around the screen (you can't drag a program group off the Program Manager window). You'll see a ghostly image of the window as you drag. When you've found the window's new resting place, release the mouse button and voilà! The window's moved. (I wish sofas were as easy!)

If a window is maximized so that it fills your screen, you won't be able to move it around. (I mean, where would it go?) Instead, click on the Restore button to restore the window to its previous size, and then move it to wherever you'd like.

If you see a message that says, **This will close your Windows session**, click on the word **Cancel**. You get this message when you close the Program Manager window, which tells Windows that you want to exit. (And you're not supposed to do that until the next section!)

Do You Feel a Draft? (Closing a Window)

When you close a program group window, it doesn't actually close—it is just minimized to an icon at the bottom of the Program Manager window. This makes closing a program group window a harmless thing. You'll learn later that closing a program window works differently, but let's take one thing at a time.

To close a program group window, you just double-click on the Control-menu box (which has a horizontal line in it and is located at the top left of the window; if you need help in identifying it, look back at the last figure). Try this now: double-click on the Control-menu box of the Word for Windows program group.

Later when we're working in Word for Windows, you'll have to be more careful. If you don't close a *program window* (that is, a window in which a program is running) correctly, you can lose the document you're working on.

When You're Done for the Day and You Want to Go Home

Here comes that logical side of me again. Since I started this chapter showing you how to get into Windows, I thought I'd end by showing you how to get out (how to exit).

To exit Windows, exit all your programs first. In other words, close all the windows that programs are running in. (This should be a moot point at the moment, since we didn't start any programs.) Then double-click on the Program Manager's Control-menu box. This will close the Program Manager window, which in turn, closes down Windows itself.

By the Way . . .

Here's an alternative procedure for closing a window: first, click once on the Control-menu box. The Control menu will open, displaying a list of choices. Click on the word **C**lose.

A message will appear, telling you that you are about to end your Windows session. Translation: "Windows is about to close down for the night. Is this OK?" If it is, click on the word **OK**. If not, click on the word **Cancel**. If you click on **OK**, you'll exit Windows and return to either your really cool menu or the boring (yawn) DOS prompt.

The Least You Need to Know

Opening windows, closing windows—I'm pretty dizzy from all the stuff we covered in this chapter. Let's look at an instant replay:

☞ To start Windows, type **WIN** at the DOS prompt.

☞ Program Manager is the main Windows program. It helps you switch between programs and customize the way your programs work with Windows.

☞ To click with a mouse, you press the left mouse button once.

☞ To double-click, you press the left mouse button twice in rapid succession.

☞ To drag, first you move the pointer to the starting position. Then you click and hold the mouse button. Drag the pointer to the ending position, and then release the mouse button.

☞ A program group is a window that contains related programs.

☞ To maximize a window, click on the Maximize button (the upward pointing arrow). To minimize a window, click on the Minimize button (the downward pointing arrow). To return a window to its original size before it was maximized, click on the Restore button (the double-headed arrow). To adjust a window to a specific size, drag its edge.

☞ To move a window, drag it by its title bar.

☞ To close a window, double-click on the Control-menu box (located in the upper-left corner of every window).

☞ To exit the Windows program, double-click on the Program Manager's Control-menu box.

Chapter 4
Getting Off to the Right Start

In This Chapter

- ☞ How to start Word for Windows
- ☞ The basic parts of a Word for Windows screen
- ☞ Choosing commands
- ☞ Navigating a dialog box with ease
- ☞ Undoing a command
- ☞ Repeating a command
- ☞ Shutting down Word for Windows safely

Telling someone what to do is kind of fun. I think that deep down, we all want to be in charge of something. This is one of the things that I like most about using a computer—I get to tell it what to do.

The thing I like *least* is learning how. Like most kids (and some adults) I know, computers love pretending they don't understand. So the trick to using a computer is to learn how to phrase things right. Once you learn that, a computer will do just about anything you tell it to (except the ironing—darn).

If you can't get the hang of double-clicking, just click one time to highlight the icon, and then press **Enter**. I used to do that all the time in place of double-clicking, until I got used to my plastic rodent.

In this chapter, you'll learn the simplest and quickest ways to tell Word for Windows what to do. But wait—as an added bonus, the skills you learn in this chapter will apply (for the most part) to all the other Windows programs you use!

Launching (Starting) Word for Windows

The steps you use to "fire the Word for Windows rocket" are the same as with any application, so what you learn here, you'll use throughout Windows. As you go through these steps, just keep thinking, "I'm smarter than this stupid hunk of metal." Of course you are, but when I was a new user, it was helpful to remember that it was the computer that was stupid, not me. So here are the steps to start Word for Windows:

Word for Windows program icon ———

Word for Windows program group window ———

Other program groups ———

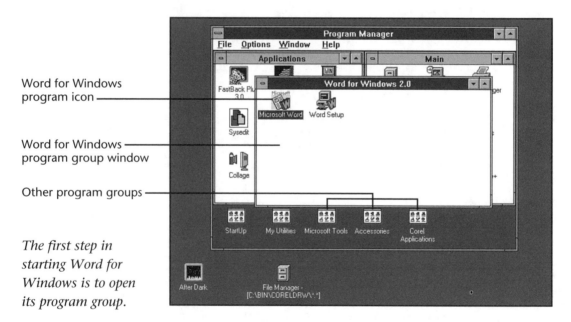

The first step in starting Word for Windows is to open its program group.

First, open the Word for Windows program group. Hey, didn't you learn to do that in the last chapter? Good timing! Just double-click on the Word for Windows program group icon.

Next, double-click on the Word for Windows program icon. Just move the pointer on top of the icon and click twice real fast. Word for Windows will start—one small step for the program, one giant step for us!

Tour de Word for Windows

Once inside the program, you'll notice some familiar friends: the Minimize, Maximize, and Restore buttons, the Control-menu box, and the title bar. Actually, you may think you're seeing double because you're seeing some things twice—but what you're really looking at is one window *inside* another. Let's look around and see what's new!

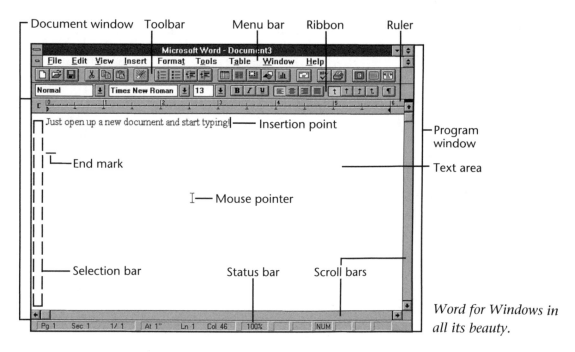

Word for Windows in all its beauty.

Program window   This is the window that Word for Windows runs in. Close this window, and you close down (exit) Word for Windows. This window frames the tools and the menus for the Word for Windows program.

Document window   This window frames the controls and information for the document file being worked on. You can have multiple document windows open at one time. (You'll learn how to open multiple document windows in Chapter 8.)

Menu bar   Displays a list of menus that contain the commands you'll use to edit documents.

Toolbar   Presents the most common commands in an easy-to-access form. For example, one of the buttons on the Toolbar saves your document when you click on it.

Ribbon   Provides an easy method for changing the appearance of text: for example, adding bold and italic.

Ruler   Provides an easy method for setting tab stops, indentations, and margins.

Scroll bars   Located along the bottom and right sides of the document window. You use scroll bars to display other areas of the document.

Status bar   Displays information about your document.

End mark   This is Word for Windows' way of marking the end of the document; as you enter text, this mark will move down.

Selection bar   This invisible area that runs along the left side of the document window provides a quick way for you to select a section of text that you want to edit.

Text area   The main part of the document window; this is where the text you type will appear.

When you work with Word for Windows, you use a default *template* (called NORMAL.DOT) that defines the working environment, such as margin settings, page orientation, and so on. The template also controls which menu commands are available and what tools appear on the Toolbar.

Word for Windows comes with additional templates that you can use to create specialized documents, and if you are using one of these templates, your screen may look different from the ones shown in this book. Also, you may have additional commands available on the menus. To see which template you are using, choose the **T**emplate... command on the **F**ile menu. If it says NORMAL under Attach **D**ocument To..., then you're using the default template.

Menu, Please

Tucked away at the top of the Word for
Windows screen, you'll see something called a
menu bar. The menu bar is like a salad bar,
except instead of choosing from carrots,
mushrooms, and radishes, you're choosing
commands.

Pull down A *pull-down*
menu contains commands
you can select. This type of
menu, when activated, is
pulled down below the
main menu bar, like a
window shade being pulled
down from the top of a
window frame.

The menu bar lists the main menus, such as
File, Edit, View, and so on. Under each of
these menus, there are additional
selections, but you can't
see them until you *pull
down* (open) the menu. (Be patient; you'll learn how to
pull one down soon.)

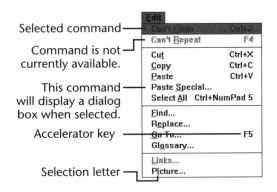

Reading the Menu

I have trouble understanding the menus in fancy
French restaurants (I took Spanish), but I'm sure
you'll have no such trouble with the Word for
Windows menu system; it follows certain conven-
tions that make it easy to understand:

Selected command ——

Command is not —
currently available.

This command ——
will display a dialog
box when selected.

Accelerator key ——

Selection letter —

Edit	
Can't Undo	Ctrl+Z
Can't Repeat	F4
Cut	Ctrl+X
Copy	Ctrl+C
Paste	Ctrl+V
Paste Special...	
Select All	Ctrl+NumPad 5
Find...	
Replace...	
Go To...	F5
Glossary...	
Links...	
Picture...	

*A typical Word for
Windows menu.*

To close a menu you opened by accident, press **Esc** or click anywhere in the document.

Grayed text   Commands that are currently unavailable will be grayed (and otherwise depressed) because you can't select them.

Selection letter   A single letter of a menu command, such as the *x* in Exit, used to activate the command from the keyboard while the menu is open. Selection letters appear as underlined letters on the main menu and as bold letters in this book.

Accelerator key   Sometimes called shortcut keys. Like selection letters, these can be used to activate the command with the keyboard. Unlike selection letters, however, accelerator keys work without opening the menu. Accelerator keys (which usually consist of a function key or key combination, such as Alt+F12) are displayed next to the menu command.

To use an accelerator key, press and hold the first key (in this case, **Alt**), and then press the second key (in this case, **F12**).

Dialog box   A dialog box is a special window that appears when the program requires additional information before it can execute a command.

Ellipsis   An ellipsis consists of three periods after a menu command, such as the File Save **As**... command. An ellipsis indicates that after this command is chosen, a *dialog box* will appear, requiring you to provide more specific information before the command is executed.

If there is an accelerator key for a command, you can press the key combination to activate the command, instead of opening the menu. For example, to select the File **S**ave command, you can press the Shift and F12 keys at the same time.

Take Your Pick: Selecting Menu Commands

It's easy to select menu commands: just point to the menu name and click. For example, click on the word File to open the File menu. While the menu is open, click once on a menu command to select it.

So that the keyboard doesn't get too jealous, I'll show you how you can use it to select commands. Press **Alt** and the selection letter to open a menu (for example, press **Alt** and F to open the File menu). Then press the selection letter alone to choose a command (for example, press X to select Exit).

By the way, if you're a former WordPerfect user, you can make Word for Windows support all those WordPerfect shortcut keys you were forced to memorize. Just use the WordPerfect Help command on the **Help** menu. In the dialog box that opens, click once on Automatic Keys. This attaches WordPerfect's values to your keyboard keys.

What's Wrong with This Picture?

```
 View
 • Normal
   Outline
   Page Layout

   Draft

 √ Toolbar
 √ Ribbon
 √ Ruler

   Header/Footer...
   Footnotes
   Annotations
   Field Codes

   Zoom...
```

Can you decipher the meaning of the check marks in front of Toolbar, Ribbon, and Ruler? And what's that dot doing in front of Normal?

Answer: The check mark is a standard way of letting you know an option is "on." The Toolbar, Ribbon, and Ruler commands are toggles that can be turned off or on (think of a light switch). Select them when the check mark is displayed, and you'll turn them "off." By the way, when the Toolbar, Ribbon, and Ruler commands are on, they appear on your screen. When they're off, they don't.

Now, what about that dot in front of the Normal command? Normal is just one way of viewing your document (Page Layout and Draft are other methods that you'll learn about in Chapter 7). The dot tells you which viewing mode you are currently using. If you were to select **Page Layout** from this menu, the dot in front of **Normal** would move to **Page Layout**.

Talking to Your Computer with Dialog Boxes

To close a dialog box without choosing anything, just press **Esc**.

When you select a menu command followed by an ellipsis, as in the File Print... command, a dialog box appears.

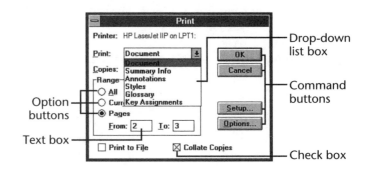

A typical dialog box.

Meet the characters that hang around dialog boxes:

List box   Presents a list of items to choose from, such as a list of files.

Drop-down list box   Like a normal list box, except that the list is not displayed until activated. The list is displayed under the main list item, much like a window shade.

Text box   Allows you to type information, such as the name of a file.

Check box   Used to indicate options that can be turned on or off, such as Collate Copies. When a check box is selected, an X appears inside it.

Option buttons   Used to select *mutually exclusive* options (options that you can select only one of), such as **A**ll, Current **P**age, or **P**ages. When an option button is selected, a dot appears inside it.

Command buttons   Perform some specific command, such as OK or Cancel.

Making the Right Choice

I like dialog boxes because they give me so many things to play with, such as list boxes and options buttons and the like. (I think it reminds me of all those pinball games I used to play as a child.) Anyway, here's how you flip all those "switches" and press all those "buzzers":

To move around a dialog box, click on any item to activate it; if you want to use the keyboard, press **Tab** until you get to the area you want. You can also press Alt and the underlined letter you see on the screen to move to a particular place within the dialog box (in this book, those underlined letters will appear as bold).

To display additional options in a list, click on the up or down arrow to scroll one item at a time and click on an item to select it. If you're using the keyboard, use the arrow keys to scroll through the list and to select an item.

To open a drop-down list box, click on the arrow to the right of the box. Click on an item to select it. With the keyboard, use the down arrow key to open the list box and to highlight an item.

To select an option button or check box, click on it to toggle the option on or off. With the keyboard, use the Spacebar to toggle an option on or off.

   You'll meet some standard command buttons while using dialog boxes (such as Cancel, which cancels the choices you have made in the dialog box and returns you to your program). If you want to close the dialog box and execute your choices, use the **OK** button. Sometimes there'll be a Close button, which retains the choices you made and closes the dialog box without executing your choices right now.

I Think Icon, I Think Icon!

The Toolbar is the quickest way for you to select the most common commands. The Toolbar hides at the top of the Word for Windows screen. The little squares that make up the Toolbar are called *buttons* because you "press" them (click on with the mouse) to select them. They are also called *icons* because they contain little pictures that represent the task they perform. Actually, some of those icons are a bit obscure, so here's a rundown of what each button is for. (You'll learn the specifics of each command in upcoming chapters, so stay tuned!)

Click on this . . .	To do this . . .
New	Open a new document.
Open	Open an existing document.
Save	Save the document you're working on.
Cut	Remove text and store it for placement elsewhere.
Copy	Copy text for placement elsewhere.
Paste	Insert stored text at current location.
Undo	Undo the last action or command.
Numbered List	Change text to numbered list style.
Bulleted List	Change text to bulleted list style.
Unindent	Move the left margin back to the previous tab stop.
Indent	Move the left margin forward to the next tab stop.
Table	Change text to table style.
Text Columns	Change text to newspaper-style columns.
Frame	Insert a frame for handling text, graphics, and tables.
Draw	Start Microsoft Draw.
Graph	Start Microsoft Graph.
Envelope	Create an envelope.
Spelling	Check the current document for spelling errors.
Zoom Whole Page	View the entire current page on-screen.
Zoom 100 Percent	View the document at its normal size.
Zoom Page Width	View the document so its full width is displayed.

Good Friends to Know: Undo and Repeat

If a command is in progress, you can press **Esc** to cancel it. But what happens if you just finished deleting some text, and it was the wrong text? I can't tell you how many times I've done just that. Well, weep no more. You can restore your deleted text with a little magic button called Undo.

 Undo undoes your last action or command. If for some reason your last action can't be undone (such as saving a document), Undo becomes unavailable. How do you undo? Just click on the **Undo** button on the Toolbar. (You learned about the Toolbar and the secret location of the Undo button in the last section.) If you're a keyboard connoisseur, press **Ctrl+Z** to activate Undo instead of using the mouse (you can also use the Undo command on the Edit menu).

Repeat lets you repeat your last action or command. Repeat lets you repeat your last action or command. I say, Repeat lets you . . . oops! (I seem to be repeating myself, which is easy to do with the Repeat command.) For example, suppose you've just changed some text so that it's bold, underlined, and 2 inches from the left margin. You can repeat this same sequence of commands on another section of text by using the Repeat command. Repeat also duplicates typing, as shown in the beginning of this paragraph. To use Repeat, press **F4** (sorry mouseketeers: there is no Repeat button on the Toolbar, but there is a **Repeat** command on the Edit menu that you could use your mouse to select).

TECHNO NERD TEACHES

You can customize the Toolbar with the commands you use most often. When you customize the Toolbar, it modifies the template you are currently working with. (If you customize the Toolbar when you are using the default template, NORMAL.DOT, the Toolbar will be changed for all documents.)

Let's say you often work with newsletters. You could create a template just for newsletters—which includes a customized Toolbar with buttons you'll need. The template also stores page margins, column markers, and so on. So by creating a newsletter template, not only will your Toolbar be set up and ready to go, but so will your document defaults (such as 1-inch margins and three newspaper-style columns)—you'll be all set to type this month's newsletter! Chapter 18 has all the details.

Exit, Stage Right

Here I am with another logic attack: since I started this chapter showing you how to start Word for Windows, I thought I'd end by showing you how to *stop* it. The technical name for stopping a program is called *exiting*. Here's what you do:

First, save whatever you're working on. If you don't, it won't be there when you come back. Computers are very literal, and unless you tell them to save something for you, they don't. You'll learn how to save your documents in Chapter 9.

Exit, stage right. Here you can exercise your own sense of style, because there are a multitude of ways to stop a program:

☞ Select the Exit command from the File menu.

☞ Double-click on the Word for Windows Control-menu box.

☞ Click once on the Word for Windows Control-menu box, and then select the Close command.

☞ Turn off the computer. Turning off the computer without exiting a program (in this case, two programs: Word for Windows and Windows itself) is the computer equivalent of taking a hammer and bashing yourself over the head. When you wake up, you're probably not going to remember what hit you, and neither will the computer. If you turn off a computer without first saving your work, it's gone. So, don't turn off a computer until you see the whites of DOS' eyes: the DOS prompt.

☞ When you've exited your program properly (see my diatribe above), you can probably turn off your computer. How can you tell if it's okay to do that? Look for the DOS prompt (it looks something like C> or C:\>). If you see a menu, choose an exit option to return to DOS, and then turn off the computer.

The Least You Need to Know

Just about everything in this chapter is the least you need to know when using any Windows program, such as Word for Windows. Most of these are what I call my Windows life-skills:

- ☞ To start any program (such as Word for Windows), open the program group its located in, and double-click the program's icon.

- ☞ To select a menu command with the mouse, open a menu by clicking on the menu name, and then click on the command you want.

- ☞ To select a menu command with the keyboard, open a menu by pressing Alt and the selection letter. Select the command you want by pressing its selection letter.

- ☞ To select an item in a dialog box with the mouse, just click on it. Click on the down arrow to open a drop-down list box, and click on an item to select it. Clicking on an option button or a check box toggles it on or off.

- ☞ To select an item in a dialog box with the keyboard, use the Tab key. Use the arrow keys to select an item from a list. Use the Spacebar to toggle option buttons and check boxes on or off.

- ☞ To undo your last command or action, click on the **Undo** button on the Toolbar, or press **Ctrl+Z**.

- ☞ To repeat a command, press **F4**.

- ☞ The Toolbar contains the most often used commands in button form. If a command doesn't exist on the Toolbar, you can add it or select it from a menu.

- ☞ To exit Word for Windows, use the **Exit** command on the **File** menu. *Be sure to save your document before you exit any program.*

This page unintentionally left blank.

Chapter 5
Getting a Little Help from Your Friends

In This Chapter

- ☛ How to get help when you need it
- ☛ Using the Help Index
- ☛ How to complete a Word tutorial

You never know when you'll need help, so getting help when you need it is what this chapter is all about. Help in Word for Windows is as varied as the people who use it. You're sure to find help in some form that you'll like.

Getting the Help You Need

Help for Word for Windows is available 24 hours a day by pressing **F1**. Help is *context-sensitive*; which in English means that Help knows what you're doing, so when you press F1, it takes you to a section that explains that specific task. For example, when you use the command to save a document, a dialog box appears, asking for more information (such as a name for the file). If you don't know what to do when the dialog box appears, just press **F1**, and you'll be taken to the section in the help system that talks about saving your document.

Help with Menus

If a menu is open and you're wondering what a particular command will do, you've got two options:

☞ Press **Shift+F1** and the mouse pointer will change to a question mark. Move the pointer to a command and click.

☞ Highlight the command with the arrow keys and press **F1**.

Help with an Area of the Screen

If you're looking at your Word for Windows screen and you're wondering, "Now, what in the world is that?" there's a way you can find out. First, press **Shift+F1** and the mouse pointer will change to a cute little question mark. Next, click on the questionable item (such as a Toolbar button or a menu command).

(Sorry, it seems that only mouse users are allowed to have questions about the Word for Windows screen.)

How Can You Find the Answer, When You're Not Sure of the Question?

When you're not sure what to do or where to start, use the **Help** menu. To open the Help menu, click on it or press **Alt+H**. When the **Help** menu is open, you'll have many things to choose from:

Help Index   This option is perfect when you have an idea of what you're looking for.

Getting Started   This tutorial is great for the first-time user. If you're new to word processing or to Word for Windows, these lessons will get you up to speed fast.

Learning Word   This tutorial is perfect for after you have learned the basics. The most popular Word for Windows tasks are presented here in a hands-on style that lets you practice the commands without affecting your document.

Product Support   Get answers to the most often asked questions. (If you don't see this option, you may not have the latest version of Word for Windows. Call the Word for Windows Help Line for information on how to receive the upgrade.)

WordPerfect Help   Switching from WordPerfect? Use this help command to get you up and running in Word.

About...   Check to see how much *memory* and *hard disk* space you have left.

Let Your Fingers Do the Walking: Using the Help Index

If you're just sitting in your document wondering how to add a page number (or some such), you can use the Help Index. To open the Index, press **F1** or select the Help Index command from the Help menu.

Memory   An electronic storage area inside the computer, used to temporarily store data or program instructions when the computer is using them. The computer's memory is erased when the power to the computer is turned off.

Hard disk   A non-removeable disk drive that stores a great quantity of data. Because it is fixed inside the computer, it operates faster and more efficiently than a floppy disk.

Click here to see a table of contents.

Click here to search for a topic.

```
─                  Word Help - WINWORD.HLP            ▲ ▼
 File   Edit   Bookmark   Help
Contents  Search  Back  History    <<        >>
   Step-by-step Instructions                         ↑

   For fast access to specific information in Help, choose the Search
   button in the Help button bar.

   -A-
   Addresses (labels)
   Aligning text
   Alphabetizing lists and text
   Annotations
   Automatic saving

   -B-
   Backup copies
   Block (selection)
   Body text
   Bold
   Bookmarks
   Borders
   Bullets and bulleted lists

   -C-
   Calculations
                                                    ↓
```

Click here to go back to any previous screen.

Click here to go back to the previous screen.

The Help Index displayed in alphabetical order.

You'll be presented with a lot of choices as you try to find information on the topic you're interested in. With a mouse, simply click on something to choose it. With the keyboard, press Tab until you highlight your choice, and then press **Enter**.

To scroll through long lists, click on either arrow on the scroll bar, or press Page Down to go forward in the list or Page Up to go back.

Would You Like Fries with That? (Choosing the Kind of Help You Want)

When you open the Index, you need to choose between two basic categories of help: step-by-step instructions for a specific task, or reference information for such things as the parts of a Word for Windows screen or error messages. If you're interested in step-by-step instructions, select either of these:

Alphabetical listing   Tasks are listed alphabetically. To find out how to add a page number, look under the P's.

Chapter listing   Tasks are organized by topic, like a book. To find out how to add a page number, look under the topic *Special Features for Documents, Headers and Footers.*

If you're interested in reference information, click on the topic you want (such as Definitions or Parts of the Word Screen).

Looking for Help in All the Right Places

If you know what you're looking for, you can search for a particular topic. With the Help Index open, click on the **Search** button, and the hunt is on!

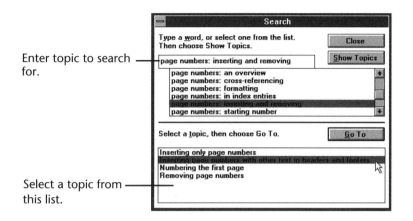

Enter topic to search for.

Select a topic from this list.

Enter the topic to search for.

Just type in the word you want to look up and press **Enter**. Related topics appear at the bottom of this dialog box. Select the topic of your choice by double-clicking on it or by using the arrow keys to highlight it and pressing **Enter**.

Put It to Work

Marking Frequently Used Topics

You can mark the topics you use most frequently so you can get to them quickly. (Think of this as putting a paper clip on a favorite page in a book.) Once you have a favorite topic displayed:

1. Open the Bookmark menu. Press **Alt+M** or click on the menu to open it.

2. Choose **Define**. Press **D** or click on **Define**.

3. If you want to change the title of the topic to something you prefer, type the topic's new name. Then press **Enter** or click on **OK**.

To get to a bookmark, open the **Help** menu by pressing **Alt+H** or by clicking on **Help**. Select Help **I**ndex by clicking on it or by pressing **I**. Then select Bookmark by pressing **Alt+M** or by clicking on the menu. When the Bookmark menu is displayed, click on a bookmark or use the arrow keys to select it.

Class Act: Using a Word Tutorial

Word tutorials take you step by step through various lessons as you learn specific Word tasks: think of them as one of those PBS do-it-yourself shows, but without the tools. You can complete a Word tutorial by using either a mouse and the keyboard or just the keyboard. First, choose either **Getting Started** or **Learning Word** from the **Help** menu. If the document you're working on has not been saved, you'll be asked if you want to save it. Press **Y** for Yes, or if you haven't really started a document yet, press **N** for No. Then select either the mouse and keyboard technique (click or press **M**) or the keyboard-only technique (press **K**).

Now Playing in Theater Two

You can select from several lesson menus (such as the **Word Screen**) in one of two ways:

- ☞ Click on the lesson menu of your choice.

- ☞ Press the underlined letter.

From a lesson menu, you choose a lesson using the same methods described here: either click on a lesson or press the underlined letter of the lesson name to select it.

Getting Your Degree

After a lesson has started, you move from screen to screen by using the arrow keys: either click on the right arrow key or press the right arrow key on the keyboard to move to the next screen. Use the left arrow key to move backward through a lesson. Word checks off each tutorial as you complete it.

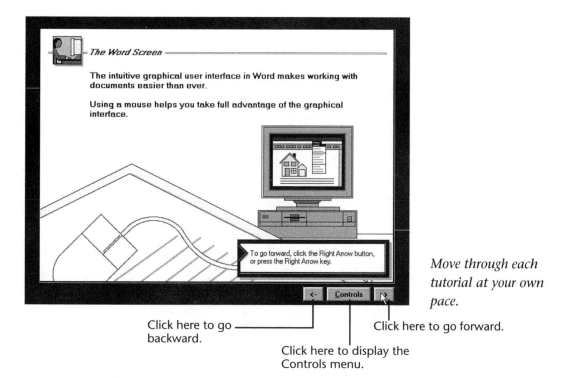

Move through each tutorial at your own pace.

Click here to go backward.

Click here to display the Controls menu.

Click here to go forward.

Through the Controls menu, you can cut class (exit), return to the lesson menu to choose another lesson, or raise your hand (get more instructions). To open the Controls menu, press **Alt+C** or click on the Controls button. From this menu, press the underlined letter of an option or click on an option to select it.

Occasionally, the tutorial will stop and let you have your turn. If you can't remember the steps necessary to complete the task, press **W** or click on Show Steps.

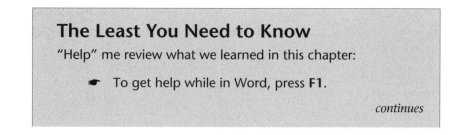

The Least You Need to Know

"Help" me review what we learned in this chapter:

☛ To get help while in Word, press **F1**.

continues

continued

☞ If you want help on a command, press **Shift+F1** and click on it, or highlight the command and press **F1**.

☞ To get help with a part of the Word screen, press **Shift+F1** and click on any item.

☞ The Help menu provides access to the Help Index and the Word tutorials.

☞ You can search for a topic by clicking on the Search button or by pressing **Alt+S** when the Help Index is open. When the Search window is displayed, type the name of the item to search for and press **Enter**. Select a topic with the arrow keys or the mouse, and away you go!

☞ Select a topic from the Help menu, then select a tutorial from subsequent menus. Use the arrow keys to move from screen to screen within the tutorial.

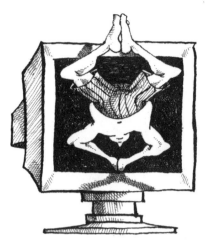

Chapter 6
Diving into a Document

In This Chapter

- ☞ Some simple rules for entering text
- ☞ Moving that darn insertion point
- ☞ Selecting the text you want to edit
- ☞ Inserting and deleting text
- ☞ Copying and moving text

Well, congratulations. You've made it to Chapter 6. Sorry about all that preliminary stuff; it seems that there's always something you have to learn before you "get down to work."

Anyway, getting down to work is what this chapter is all about—how to enter text (and how to change it once it's been entered).

Dancing Fingers: How to Enter Text into a Word Document

When you start Word for Windows, it automatically places your cursor at the top of an empty document window so that you are ready to start entering text. (The *insertion point* is a vertical line that acts like the tip of a pencil; anything you type appears at the insertion point, or cursor.) To enter text, simply start typing. As you type, your words will appear on the screen, like words from a typewriter. However, unlike using a typewriter, *you should not press Enter at the end of every line.*

By the Way . . .

The horizontal line you see on-screen is the end-of-file marker. It appears at the bottom of your file. When you start a document, there aren't any words yet, so the end-of-file marker is at the top. As you insert text, it will move down the page.

Word wrap With word wrapping, words are automatically advanced to the next line of a paragraph when they "bump" into the right-hand margin. Likewise, you can insert words into the middle of a paragraph, and the rest of the paragraph will be automatically adjusted downward. If you change the margins, paragraphs will adjust automatically.

Make appropriate mouth noises as you read this line: Word-for-Windows-will-automatically-advance-your-text-to-the-next-line-at-the-appropriate-point. This is called Word Rap; I mean *word wrap*.

But What If I Make a Mistake?

Correcting typing mistakes in Word for Windows is easy. Simply press the **Backspace** key to back up and erase text, or select unwanted text (selecting text is covered in the next section) and remove that text by pressing the **Delete** key.

Rules of the Road

Using a word processor is different from using a typewriter in many respects. So before you take Word for Windows out for a test drive, here are some rules of the road:

Don't press Enter/Return at the end of every line. I've said it before, but it's worth saying again: when you use a typewriter, you press the carriage return at the end of a line so you can move down to the next one. When you use a word processor and your text bumps into the right margin, the word processor grabs the last word on that line and places it at the beginning of the next line automatically. Press **Enter** *only when you reach the end of a paragraph, or to insert a blank line.* If you want to divide an existing paragraph into two, move the cursor to the dividing point and press **Enter**. If you forget and press Enter at the end of a line, you'll create two paragraphs. To put two paragraphs together, move to the first letter of the second paragraph and press Backspace.

Use the Spacebar to insert a space between words or sentences. Don't use the Spacebar to move the cursor. (You'll learn how to move the cursor in the next section.)

Paragraph Any grouping of words that should be treated as a unit. This includes normal paragraphs as well as single line paragraphs, such as chapter titles, section headings, and captions for charts or other figures. When you press Enter in Word for Windows, you are marking the end of a paragraph.

Press Tab (not the Spacebar) to indent the first line of a paragraph. Spaces are not just blank holes on the page; they are characters. Depending on the size of the characters you're using throughout your document, your paragraphs can come out looking uneven if you use the Spacebar to align them. Using the Tab key allows Word for Windows to line up paragraphs for you.

A dotted line marks the end of a page. Just ignore the dotted line; it tells Word for Windows where one page ends and another begins. If you add text above a dotted line, the excess text at the bottom of that page will flow onto the next page automatically. You can force the end of a page by pressing **Ctrl+Enter**. (When you do this, the dots in the dotted line get denser to denote that this is a forced page break.)

Magic Trick: Moving the Insertion Point Without Entering Text

As you type, the little insertion point, or cursor, moves along with you, like a happy puppy at your heels. But suppose you want to insert (or delete, or copy, or move) a word in a previous paragraph? Do you have to back up using the Backspace key and erase everything you've done, so you can retype that sentence? The answer is a welcome "No."

What you do instead is move the insertion point. To move the insertion point with the mouse, just click on the spot where you want to move. (If you need to scroll through your document to get to the right spot, see the next chapter for some hints on scrolling.)

For People Who Let Their Fingers Do the Walking

Sometimes I hate to have my fingers leave the keyboard because they always land back on the wrong keys, and then I end up typing garbage. Here's how you can move the insertion point, and not your fingers:

To move . . .	Press . . .
Up or down one line	Up or down arrow key
Left or right one character	Left or right arrow key
One word left or right	Ctrl+ either the left or right arrow key
Up or down one paragraph	Ctrl+ either the up or down arrow key
Up or down one screen	Page Up or Page Down
Top of the screen	Ctrl+Page Up
Bottom of the screen	Ctrl+Page Down
Beginning of the line	Home
End of the line	End
Beginning of document	Ctrl+Home
End of document	Ctrl+End

By the Way . . .

You can return to a previous editing spot by using Go Back. Pressing **Shift+F5** will return you to your previous editing position up to three times.

Selecting Text

As you edit your documents, you'll probably begin by modifying only certain sections of text. For example, you may want to move a sentence from the beginning of a paragraph to the end. You can move, copy, delete, and replace text by selecting that text and then performing certain commands.

Mousing Around

To select text with the mouse, place the mouse pointer on the first letter in the text to be selected, and click. Then drag the mouse until you reach the end of the text you want to select. Release the mouse button, and the text you selected will be highlighted in reverse video.

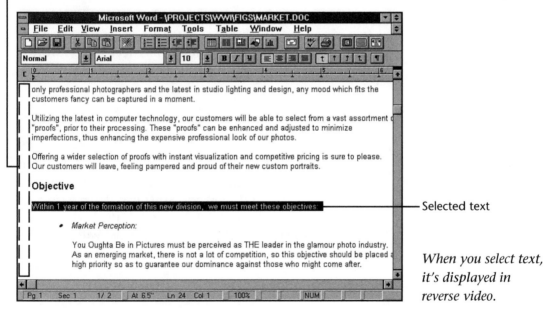

When you select text, it's displayed in reverse video.

If you find this method of selecting text a drag, here are some shortcuts you can use when selecting text with the mouse:

Text to select	Action
Word	Double-click on the word.
Sentence	Press the Ctrl key and click on the sentence.
Paragraph	Double-click in the selection bar next to the paragraph.
Multiple paragraphs	Click in the selection bar next to the first paragraph, then drag.
Line	Click in the selection bar next to the line.
Multiple lines	Drag in the selection bar next to the lines.
Whole document	Press the Ctrl key and click anywhere in the selection bar.

To extend your text selection to include more than one word, sentence, or paragraph, simply drag the pointer. For example, to select several words, double-click on one word and drag the pointer over the rest of the words you want to select.

Surf's Up, Grab Your Keyboard, and Come On!

Your keyboard is beginning to think I don't like it, so I'll show you how to select text with the keyboard too. First, move the insertion point to the first letter in the text to be selected, and press the **Shift** key. Then with the Shift key depressed, use the arrow keys to reach the end of the text you wish to select. Release the Shift key, and the text you selected will be highlighted in reverse video.

If you want to select the entire document, press **Ctrl+5** (use the 5 on the numeric keypad).

Change Your Mind?

Select the wrong text? Don't worry—just press an arrow key or click anywhere in the document. You can also select other text instead.

In with the Good: Inserting Text

Text is always inserted into a document beginning at the *insertion point* (cursor). What you type appears at the insertion point. To move the insertion point, simply click at the point where you want to begin inserting text, or use the arrow keys.

When you type text into a document, Word assumes that you want to insert text, and not type over existing text. Therefore, Word automatically uses Insert mode, in which the text you type appears at the insertion point, and all existing text is pushed to the right. However, if you do want to type over existing characters, you can turn on *Overtype mode.*

Insert mode   The default typing mode. When you are in Insert mode, the characters you type will be inserted to the right of the insertion point (cursor).

Overtype mode   The opposite of Insert mode. When you are in Overtype mode, the characters you type will replace existing characters in the document.

To toggle between Overtype and Insert mode, press the **Insert** key. If you are in Overtype mode, OVR appears at the bottom of the screen on the Status bar. Remember that the default is Insert mode. When you place the insertion point in text and start typing, words are inserted at that point. To type over (replace) existing text, use OVR mode (overtype).

Well, thank goodness we got through that! From now on, the only mode I want to think about is apple pie a la *mode*.

Out with the Bad: Deleting Text

Deleting text is the opposite of inserting. To delete a section of text:

☞ Select the text you wish to delete.

☞ Press the **Delete** key.

You can also delete text as you type by backing up with the **Backspace** key.

But I Didn't Mean to Delete That!

 Everyone has a right to change their mind (being a woman, I've always contended that I have more right to do that than anyone else). If you find that you've deleted some text you meant to save, select Edit from the main menu and choose Undo. As long as the Undo command is not grayed (meaning that you can't select it), you'll undo your most recent action. You can also click on the **Undo** button on the Toolbar to undo your previous action.

Copying and Moving Text

Copying and moving text is often the key to "fine-tuning" a document. Because of this, the techniques you'll learn in this section will probably be the ones that you use the most. When text is copied or moved, the Windows *Clipboard* is used.

Copy Cat!

To copy text, "copy" these steps: first, select the text that you want to copy using the methods you learned earlier in this chapter. Then open the Edit menu and choose Copy. The text is copied to the Clipboard.

Next, move the pointer to the place where you want to insert the text, and click to establish the insertion point. Open the Edit menu again and this

SPEAK LIKE A GEEK

Clipboard The Windows Clipboard is a special area inside your computer where data is stored temporarily as it is moved or copied from one place to another. Think of the Clipboard as a kind of invisible way station for data. Using the Clipboard area, a Windows program such as Word for Windows can copy data from within the same document, from one document to another, *and also to or from another Windows program.*

time choose **Paste**. The text is copied from the Clipboard into the document at the insertion point.

Copying in the Fast Lane

There are some shortcuts you can use to save time copying:

 To copy text, select it and press **Ctrl+C**, or click on the **Copy** button on the Toolbar.

 To paste text, press **Ctrl+V** or click on the **Paste** button.

To place the same section of text in multiple areas of a document, simply repeat the Edit Paste command. The contents of the Clipboard are never erased (until you exit Windows); they are replaced. As long as you have not copied something else to the Clipboard with the Edit Copy command, whatever you originally copied is still there, waiting to be pasted over and over again.

Moving Day

Moving text is very similar to copying. Move along with me here: first, select the text that you want to move using the methods you learned earlier in this chapter. Then open the Edit menu and select **Cut**. The text is moved to the Clipboard.

Then move the pointer to the place where you want to insert the text, and click to establish the insertion point. Open the Edit menu again, and choose **Paste**. The text is moved from the Clipboard into the document at the insertion point.

When you use the Cut command, the selected text is removed from the document and placed on the Clipboard. If something else is copied to the Clipboard before you finish moving the text, the text that you selected to be moved will be lost.

Get a Move On with These Fast Techniques

Here are some shortcuts you can use to save time moving text:

 To move (cut) text, select it and press **Ctrl+X**, or click on the **Cut** button on the Toolbar.

 To paste text, press **Ctrl+V** or click on the **Paste** button on the Toolbar.

> ### By the Way . . .
>
> When I want to move text to a place I can see on-screen, I just drag and drop text where I want it to be. To move text with the mouse, select it and then click and hold the left mouse button. The cursor will change to an arrow with a little rectangle below it. Drag that pointer to the place where you want to insert the text, and then release the button. The selected text is moved to the insertion point. By the way, you can copy text by pressing **Ctrl** as you drag.

I Like Spike!

If you need to make major changes to your document by moving several sections of text to one spot, save time with Spike. Here's how it works: first, select an item to move. Then to move the item to Spike, press **Ctrl+F3**. Repeat this process as much as you need to, gathering up pieces you want to move. Unlike the Clipboard, your next selection is added to the existing text in the Spike, instead of replacing it.

Once you have all the text you want to move within the Spike, move the insertion point, and then press **Ctrl+Shift+F3**. This will empty the Spike and place its contents at the current location. If you don't want to empty the Spike (because you want to insert it in more than one place, for example), type the word **spike** at the insertion point and press **F3**. The contents of the Spike are placed here, but the Spike is not emptied. With this method, you can copy the contents of the Spike to several locations within the document.

The Least You Need to Know

Editing is the heart of creating any kind of document with a word processor, so here's a quick review of what you'll need to know to make your documents perfect:

☛ Text is entered at the cursor, otherwise known as the insertion point.

☛ To enter text using a word processor, don't press Enter—except at the end of a paragraph. Don't use the Spacebar—except once between words and once or twice between sentences. Use the **Tab** key, not the Spacebar, to indent paragraphs.

☛ To end a page before it is full, press **Ctrl+Enter**.

☛ To move the insertion point with the mouse, just click on the place where you want to move it.

☛ To select text with the mouse, press and hold the mouse button and drag the mouse over the text. To select text with the keyboard, press and hold the **Shift** key as you use the arrow keys to highlight the text.

☛ The Insert key toggles between Insert mode and Overtype mode.

☛ To delete text, select it and press **Delete**.

☛ To copy text quickly, select it and press **Ctrl+C** or use the **Copy** button. Paste text in a new location by pressing **Ctrl+V** or by clicking on the **Paste** button.

☛ To move text quickly, select it and press **Ctrl+X** or use the **Cut** button. Paste text in a new location by pressing **Ctrl+V** or by clicking on the **Paste** button.

☛ To move several sections of text to one location, select each section of text and press **Ctrl+F3** in turn. When you're ready to place the text, press **Ctrl+Shift+F3**.

This page unintentionally left blank.

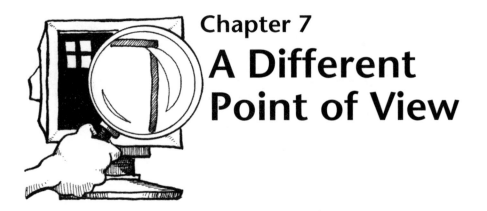

Chapter 7
A Different Point of View

In This Chapter

- ☛ The many ways you can view your document
- ☛ Viewing your document before you print
- ☛ Moving back and forth through a document

This chapter is all about points of view: what you see on your screen when you look at your document and, more importantly, *what you don't see.* There is a perfect document view for each of the tasks you are trying to accomplish: editing (Normal view), manipulating graphics or pictures (Page Layout view), or preparing to print (Print Preview).

A Word Horse: Normal View

The default viewing mode for Word for Windows is a little word (or work) horse called (aptly enough) Normal. Normal view is the best all-purpose view mode for working. But even Normal view is not totally "normal"; it has some interesting quirks that you should be aware of.

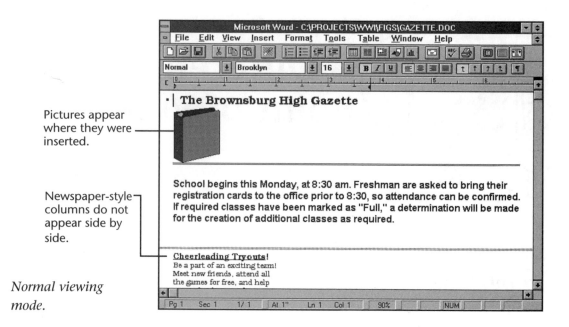

Pictures appear where they were inserted.

Newspaper-style columns do not appear side by side.

Normal viewing mode.

Newspaper-style columns Similar columns found in newspapers. Text flows between invisible boundaries down one part of the page. When the text hits the end of a column, it wraps to the top of the next.

Frames Small boxes in which you place text or pictures so you can easily maneuver them within your document.

Headers and footers A header is text that will be repeated at the top of every page, and a footer is text that will be repeated at the bottom.

Newspaper-style columns do not appear side by side as they will appear on the printed paper. Instead, they appear as one continuous column. You'll learn how to create *newspaper-style columns* in Chapter 20.

Pictures and text that you've placed in frames will appear where they are first inserted into the document, not where they will be when printed. You'll learn how to work with *frames* in Chapter 21.

When you add headers, footers, or footnotes, you work in a separate dialog box, outside of the regular document. You'll learn more about *headers and footers* in Chapter 13.

Switching to Normal View

To switch to Normal view from some other view, open the View menu and select Normal. Pretty easy, huh?

How to Speed Up Normal View

As you move back and forth through your document, the computer is constantly redrawing what is being displayed on your screen. Think of trying to do a pencil sketch of a tennis match: although a computer is very fast, if your document contains complex graphics (pictures) or other detailed information, this redrawing process can take longer than you'd like.

While using Normal view, you can speed up the redraw process by switching to Draft Normal mode. Just open the View menu and select **Draft** (if you open the View menu again, you'll see a little check mark in front of Draft; that means it's working).

What You See Is Almost What You Get: Page Layout View

If you've been working in Normal view and you want to see such things as columns, graphics, or headers as they will appear when printed, switch to Page Layout view.

The only elements that don't appear in Page Layout view are line numbers (like those found in legal documents) and lines between columns. These are small items and not things you're likely to notice, but if it's important that you see everything that will print on your final document, use the Print Preview view discussed later in this chapter.

By the Way . . .

One important difference between these two views: Page Layout view allows you to continue editing, while Print Preview limits you to global, earth-shattering changes like margin settings.

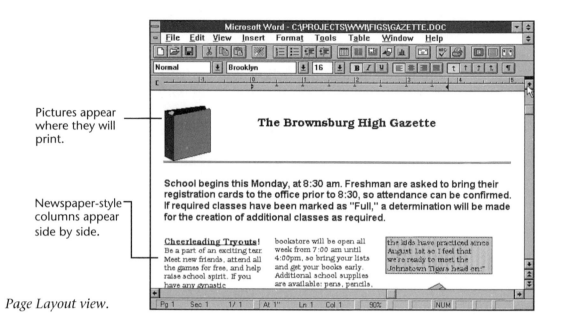

Pictures appear where they will print.

Newspaper-style columns appear side by side.

Page Layout view.

No viewing mode is perfect—but don't worry, there is an appropriate mode for each task you are trying to accomplish. Here are some quirks about the Page Layout view that you should be aware of:

Use this mode to work with frames. You'll see the text and graphic "boxes" as they'll appear when printed, so you can use this mode to create, edit, and resize frames.

When you scroll your document, you move through the document one whole page at a time. You can't display the bottom half of one page and the top half of another in Page Layout view.

When working with headers, footers, and footnotes, you work in the document, not in a separate box as you do in Normal view.

Making the Switch to Page Layout View

Make the switch—here's how: just open the View menu and choose **Page Layout.** (Click on the View menu or press **Alt+V**, then click on **Page Layout** or press **P**.)

Look Before You Print: Using Print Preview

Unlike Normal or Page Layout view, when you use Print Preview view, *everything* is displayed as it will print. Also, if you like what you see, you can print your document by simply clicking on the **Print** button.

You can't use Print Preview to make editing changes, because it would be too difficult to see what you're doing. There's all this really teeny text, you see, and if you put it under a magnifying glass you still couldn't read it because it looks like a three-thousand-year-old excavated mosaic from the Libraries of Alexandria. You can, however, use Print Preview to make broad changes, such as margin settings.

Click here to see two pages at once.

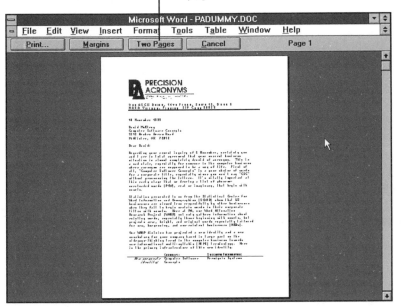

Print Preview view.

If You Switch Right Now, We'll Give You One Month's Free Service . . .

To switch to Print Preview view, just open the View menu and select Print Preview. (I bet that View menu is getting awfully familiar by now.)

To change to Page Layout view from here, double-click in an area of the screen that's off the page(s). To return to the previous view you were using, click on the Close or Cancel button. You can display two pages at a time by clicking on the Two Pages button. Toggle back to a single page display by clicking on the One Page button.

Changing Margin Settings in Print Preview View

This is one of the few changes you can make while in Print Preview view, so I thought I'd give it special treatment: its own section. To change the margins, click on the Margins button, then drag a margin handle to its new location (point at the margin handle and press and hold the left mouse button as you move the mouse).

Magnifying What You See

Sherlock Holmes would have loved this option. In both Normal and Page Layout views, you can adjust the page display as if you were holding a magnifying glass to the screen. With the touch of a button, you can choose from several magnifications as described below. It's elementary, my dear Watson:

 Zoom Whole Page   Use this button to see an entire page of your document on the screen.

 Zoom 100 Percent   Use this button to see your document in its normal size.

Zoom Page Width   Use this button to see both margins of your document on the screen. When you use this mode, the text fills the screen from side to side. I call this the "Large Print" view; it's great for people like me who have trouble seeing words after working on a computer all day.

You can also choose to see your document at twice its normal size (200%), half its normal size (50%), and three-quarters of its normal size (75%) by using the Zoom command on the View menu. Just click on the commands or press **Alt+V** to open the View menu, then press **Z** for Zoom.

Taking Your Document Out for a Scroll

When I'm editing, I tend to move around the document a lot: making changes, reading, and rereading, until I find just the right words or just the right look. Such jumping around is called *scrolling*. You can move through a document (scrolling) by using a mouse or the keyboard.

The fastest way to scroll through a document is with the mouse and the scroll bars. You'll find the vertical scroll bar lurking along the right-hand side of the document window. This scroll bar looks like an elevator shaft with a tiny elevator suspended in it. That "elevator" is called the *scroll box*, and its position within the entire scroll bar tells you roughly where you are within your document. For example, if the scroll box is close to the bottom of the scroll bar, then you're almost at the end of your document.

You'll also see a scroll bar along the bottom of the window; it's called the horizontal scroll bar, and it tells you where you are in relation to the margins of your document. The following list tells you how to take your document "out for a scroll."

Scroll bars

Scroll box

Scroll arrow

You move through your document with a scroll bar and a mouse.

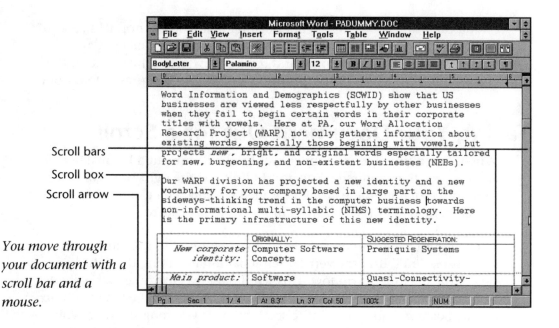

To move . . .	Click . . .
Up or down one line	On the up or down arrow of the vertical scroll bar.
Left or right one character	On the left or right arrow of the horizontal scroll bar.
Up or down one screen	Above or below the scroll box in the right-hand scroll bar.
A portion of the document length	On the vertical scroll box and drag it up or down a proportionate amount.
A portion of the document width	On the horizontal scroll box, and drag it left or right a proportionate amount.
In Normal view, past the zero mark on the ruler	On the left arrow on the horizontal scroll bar while holding down the Shift key.

Most Windows programs do not display the scroll bars unless there is some portion of your document that is not being displayed (for example, if the right margin is hidden, you would see a horizontal scroll bar that you could use to scroll right). Word for Windows does not follow this unwritten rule; instead, it displays both the horizontal and vertical scroll bars at all times, unless you turn them off. Okay, there are exceptions to every rule, and this time it's Print Preview. When you're in Print Preview, the horizontal scroll bar does not display—probably because you use the Page Down key to move right (to the next page).

Anyway, back to what I was saying: to turn the scroll bars off, open the Tools menu and select **Options**. Under Category, select View. In the Window area, use the horizontal or vertical scroll bar check boxes to toggle the scroll bars on or off. When you're done making your choices, click on **OK**.

Scrolling with the Keyboard

To scroll through a document with the keyboard, simply press **Page Down** to move one screen forward in the document. Press **Page Up** to move one screen back. You can get nowhere fast by scrolling one line at a time with the Up and Down arrow keys.

Unlike when you use the mouse with the scroll bar, scrolling with the keyboard *does* move the insertion point, so you don't have to unpack your editing bags when you get there—you're ready to edit.

Keep in mind that scrolling with the mouse simply changes the part of the document you're looking at. If you want to start editing, click within the document to move the insertion point. If you missed the award-winning documentary "Magic Trick: Moving the Insertion Point Without Entering Text" when it was on TV, see Chapter 6 for a quick review.

I know it's weird that the Page keys don't move you one whole *page* in your document (like from page 1 to page 2), but the computer's "page" is its screen, so that's why the keys work that way.

What's Wrong with This Picture?

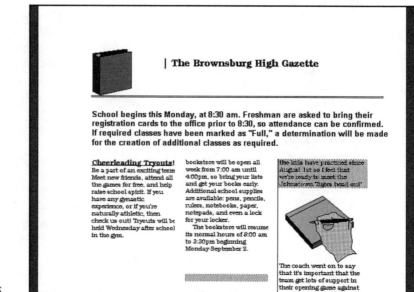

The Case of the Disappearing Menus.

Take a good look at this picture. Can you list everything that's missing?

Answer: If you said the scroll bars, the menu bar, the Toolbar, Ruler, and Ribbon, you're right. If these things are just a collection of junk that gets in the way of your typing, get rid of them! In Word for Windows, you have the option of removing everything from the screen so you can do your typing in peace. This option will be especially welcome if you switched from WordPerfect, where the normal operating environment does not include any clutter.

So, whether you're a former WordPerfect user, or you just want to give this a try, here's what you do: open the Tools menu and select Options. Under Category, select View. Then select the Full Screen check box.

To return to "normal" clutter, just press **Esc** anytime you want.

The Least You Need to Know

Depending on your "point of view," these may or may not be the highlights of this chapter. Here goes:

- ☞ Use Normal view for normal editing tasks. Select **View Normal**.

- ☞ Speed up Normal view by adding the **D**raft option. Select **View D**raft.

- ☞ Page Layout view is great for working with graphics. You can see just about everything as it will look when you print it, and you can still make changes to your document. Select **View P**age Layout.

- ☞ Use Print Preview just prior to printing, or to make broad changes, such as margin settings. Select **File** Print Preview.

- ☞ Want to see something close-up? Use any of the Zoom options on the **View** menu.

- ☞ To see something in another part of your document, scroll with the scroll bars and a mouse.

- ☞ If you want to scroll using the keyboard, press **Page Up** or **Page Down** or use the arrow keys.

- ☞ If you want to remove everything from your screen but the text area, use the **Tools O**ptions command.

This page unintentionally left blank.

Chapter 8
Juggling Documents

In This Chapter

- Creating a new document
- Opening an existing document
- Returning to a previous editing position within a document
- Finding little lost documents
- "Paneless" ways to work with multiple documents
- Working in two places in a document at the same time

Maybe it's not so wonderful to have to juggle multiple projects and changing priorities, but at least Word for Windows works the way we really do: that is, *on more than one thing at a time.* As you work in Word for Windows, you'll find yourself opening old documents and starting new ones. You may even want to have several documents showing on your screen at the same time or to display two parts of the same document at the same time. This chapter will show you how to do all this and more.

Starting A-New

When you first start Word for Windows, it assumes you want to start something new, so it accommodates you by giving you a blank screen. But what do you do when you've just finished one document, and you want to start "a-new"? How do you get an empty window so you can start typing?

Well, you've got two options:

- ☛ Open the File menu and select the New command. Just click to open the menu and select the command, or press **Alt+F** and then **N**. A dialog box will open. You can basically ignore this box and press **Enter** unless you want to base this document on a template other than the Normal template.

- ☛ Click on the **New** button on the Toolbar. This is the quickest method if you have a mouse and you want to base your new document on the NORMAL template. If you want to select another template, you must use the New command on the File menu.

When you work with Word for Windows, you use a default *template* (called NORMAL.DOT) that defines margin settings, page orientation, and so on. Word for Windows comes with additional templates (see Chapter 18) that you can use to create specialized documents, such as memos, proposals, overheads, faxes, and mailing labels. If you want to use one of these specialized templates, use the **File New** command.

What's Wrong with This Picture?

Yvonne wants to create a memo using the MEMO2 template, so she clicks on the New button on the Toolbar to start a new document. What did Yvonne do wrong?

Answer: She should **have** used the New command on the File menu and selected the MEMO2 template from the dialog box that was displayed. When she clicked on the New button on the Toolbar, Word assumed that she wanted to use the NORMAL template to create a new document, and it didn't display the dialog box.

Document Déjà Vu: Opening an Existing Document

Word remembers the last four documents you worked on so that you can get to them easily. So if the document you want to work on (open) is a recent one, it'll be displayed at the end of the File menu. To open it, open the File menu and click on it or press the number next to the document name. I use this method to open existing documents more often than any other method.

If you haven't worked on a document in a while, you'll have to open it the long way.

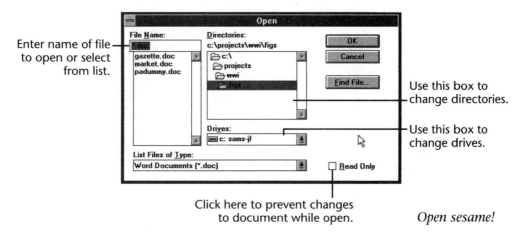

Enter name of file to open or select from list.

Use this box to change directories.

Use this box to change drives.

Click here to prevent changes to document while open.

Open sesame!

 Open the File menu and select the **Open** command, or click on the **Open** button on the Toolbar. Another one of those boxes will appear (oh goody). Either type the name of the file you want to open, or scroll through the list. Use the scroll bars or the arrow keys to scroll along.

If you can't find your file, change to a different drive or *directory*. Select a different *disk drive* from the drop-down list box by clicking on the down arrow and then clicking on a different drive. If you need to change to another directory, click on that directory.

OOPS!

When you open a foreign-format document, such as a WordPerfect file, Word attempts to convert it. Expect to lose some formatting; no conversion process is absolutely perfect.

Disk drive   A type of computer storage that reads and writes on a magnetic film. Think of a disk drive as a cassette recorder/player. Just as the cassette player can record sounds on a magnetic cassette tape and play back those sounds, a disk drive can record data on a magnetic film and play back that data. Most computers have two types of disk drives: a *hard disk drive*, which stores vast amounts of data on permanently mounted disks, and a *floppy disk drive*, which records smaller amounts of data on portable disks.

Directory   Because large hard disks can store thousands of files, you often need to store related files in separate directories on the disk. Think of your disk as a filing cabinet and think of each directory as a drawer in the filing cabinet. Keeping files in separate directories makes it easier to locate and work with related files.

If you're trying to open a document that was created in another program (such as WordPerfect), select a file type from the drop-down list box by clicking on the down arrow and then picking a type. If your file type is not listed, select **All Files**.

To protect this document against accidental changes, use the **Read Only** check box. When you're done making choices, select **OK** to open the file.

Get Back to Where You Left Off

A real nifty feature of Word for Windows is its ability to locate the place in your document where you were last working. (Now if it could only find my keys.) After you open an existing document, you can go back to where you left off by using Go Back. Just press **Shift+F5**. (You may remember Go Back from Chapter 6.) By using this handy feature, you can return to your last three editing positions within the document.

Help! I Lost My File!

If you're having trouble locating an old document, don't worry—be happy! Word has a nice command called Find File that'll do *most* of the work of locating a file for you (okay, you do have to tell it what to look for).

 First, wait 24 hours to be sure that the file is really missing and hasn't just run away. (Oops, just kidding.) Then open the File menu and select the Find File command, or if you're in the Open dialog box, click on the Find File button or press **Alt+F**.

Select a file.

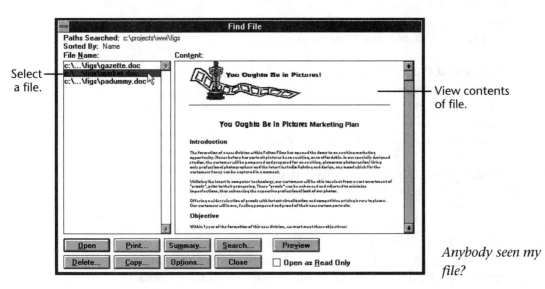

View contents of file.

Anybody seen my file?

Just the Facts, Ma'am: Telling Word What to Search For

Word displays all the .DOC files in the current directory. You can change the search criteria with the Search button. This box looks pretty complicated, but don't worry: you'll probably enter stuff in only one or two places.

Enter file name here.

Change drives and directories to search.

Enter information to use to find the file.

Enter information about the file you want to find.

File Name   If you know the name of the file to search for, enter it here. If you're not sure of the spelling, use a question mark in place of a single character, such as CHAPTER?.DOC. You can use an asterisk to replace multiple characters, as in CH*.DOC or M*.*. You'll learn more than you'll ever want to know about file names in Chapter 9.

Drives and Path   These control which disk drive and directories are searched. Ignore these—it's easier to use the Edit Path button. After clicking on Edit Path, select a different disk drive from the Drives drop-down list box. If you need to change to another directory, click on that directory. When you're done, select the **Close** button.

Title, Subject, Keywords, and Author   This information is found on the Summary Info box that you complete when you save a file. Curious? See Chapter 9.

Any Text   This matches text within a document. If you want to match case (search for "BOGUS" but not "bogus"), type the word exactly as it appears in the document, then select the Match Case check box. This should only be used with other search criteria—otherwise, the list of files to search would be huge, and the search would take a long time.

Saved By   Word for Windows saves the name of the person who last edited a document. (This assumes that the person filled in their name in the Summary Info box when they saved the file.)

Date Created and Date Saved   Enter a date using a two-digit month, day, year, as in 04/08/93.

Options   With Create New List, you create a new search pattern based on current selections. If you choose Add Matches to List, you can combine this search request with previous ones to create a wider search pattern. If you choose Search Only in List, the current list is whittled down to those files that match the current criteria too.

> ## By the Way . . .
>
> I like to change the sort options for the file list when I'm searching for files based on date or author name, and you can too. Just use the **O**ptions button in the Find File box to sort the file list by file name (default), author, creation date, save name, save date, and file size.

Once You've Found a File, Never Let It Go

Some enchanted evening, you may find your strange file, you may find your strange file across a crowded disk . . . but what can you do with a file once you've found it? Well, just about anything. You can open, print, copy, and delete any files you select. Here's how:

First, select a file or files. Use the arrow keys or click on a file to select it. The file will be displayed in the Content box. To select multiple files with the mouse, hold down the **Ctrl** key as you click on a file name. To select multiple files with the keyboard, press **Shift+F8**, and then use the arrow keys to highlight a file. With a file highlighted, press the **Spacebar** to select it.

Then select the option you want. Choose the **Open**, **Delete**, **Print**, or **Copy** button. To display the summary information on a file, use the **Summary** button. If you're copying files, enter the directory to which you want to copy the files.

What's Wrong with This Picture?

Bob wants to print two files, BUDGET.DOC and APRSALES.DOC. He opens the File menu and selects the Print command. Then he tries to select both files for printing. What did Bob do wrong?

Answer: Nothing much—he just used the wrong command. Word is perfectly capable of printing several documents in a row while you go get some coffee. Bob should have used the Find File command on the File menu to select his two files. After clicking on the Print button, Bob's off to the break room in no time!

A Paneless Way to Work with Multiple Windows

You can open up to nine documents at one time, with each of your "children" running around in its own document window. You can open them one at a time throughout a work session, or you can open several files at once by using the Find File command as explained earlier.

Active document   The document you are currently working in. The active document contains the insertion point, and if more than one document window is being displayed on-screen, the active document's title bar appears darker than those of other document windows.

Once several documents are open, you can copy or move text between them, or simply refer to one document as you edit another. You can scroll through each document and make changes as you would at any other time. However, you can only make changes to one document at a time—the *active document*.

Doing the Document Shuffle

Normally, the active document takes up the entire screen, but you can split the screen equally between all active documents by opening the **W**indow menu and selecting Arrange All. Jump between documents using one of these two methods:

Use the Window menu. Open the Window menu and select the document from the list displayed at the bottom.

OR

If more than one window is displayed on-screen, click inside a window to make it active. You can also press **Alt+F6** to move back and forth between windows.

You close document windows in the normal way, by saving the file, then closing the window. You'll learn how to do this in the next chapter.

Looking at Two Parts of the Same Document Is Not a Pane

Sometimes you want to work in two sections of the same document at the same time. For example, if you wanted to move or copy text within a long document, scrolling back and forth would be a waste of time. Instead, just split the document window into two *panes* (two sections).

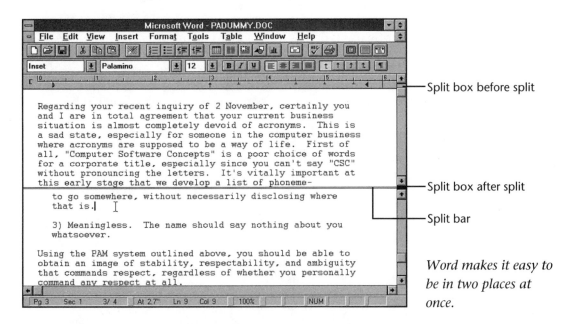

Split box before split

Split box after split

Split bar

Word makes it easy to be in two places at once.

If you've got a mouse, just double-click on the split box. This splits the window into two equal panes. If you want to adjust the sizes of the windows, drag (click the left mouse button and hold it down as you move the mouse) the split box to the desired size. To return to a single window, double-click on the split box again.

If you want to use the keyboard, open the **Window** menu and select the Arrange All command. This splits the window into two equal panes. If you want to adjust the sizes of the windows, open the document's Control menu by pressing **Alt** and the hyphen (–). Select Split and then use the arrow keys to adjust the size. Press **Enter** when the panes are the size you want. To return to a single window, use the Split command and the arrow keys to move the split bar off the window and press **Enter**.

To move between the two panes, click inside a pane to make it active, or press **F6** to toggle back and forth. You can get really fancy and select different views (see Chapter 7 for more information) for each pane.

Put It to Work

Working with a Long Document

Let's practice some of the techniques we learned in this chapter by using one of the standard documents Word comes with, the README.DOC. This is a real document that you should read sometime because it contains updates to information contained in the manual. While we're working with it, we won't make any permanent changes so you'll still have a chance to read it later.

First, let's open it. I'm taking a wild guess, but I'm going to assume that you haven't been working on this file lately, so we won't find it listed at the end of the **File** menu. This means that we're going to have to open the file manually, with the **File O**pen command. Click on the **Open** button on the Toolbar, or press **Alt+F** and then **O** to select the **O**pen command.

One of those wonderful boxes appears. The README.DOC file is in the \WINWORD directory, so if you see it listed, select it. If you're not in the right directory, we're going to have to change to the \WINWORD directory, so hang on. Either scroll through the **Directories** list to locate \WINWORD and then click on it, or press **Tab** until **Directories** is highlighted, and then use the down arrow key to change to the \WINWORD directory.

Now that you're in the right directory, select the README.DOC file. Choose **OK** to open the file. Now we're getting somewhere! Let's split the window in half:

Double-click on the split box or use the **Arrange All** command on the **Window** menu.

Now let's practice moving back and forth:

Click on either pane to activate it or press **F6** to toggle back and forth.

You can practice copying text between the two panes, but be sure *not* to save the file. When you're ready to unsplit the window, double-click on the split box again, or press **Alt+–** (hyphen) to open the Control menu. Then press **T** to select the Split command, use the arrow keys to move the split bar off the window, and press Enter. To close up, double-click on the Control-menu box or press **Ctrl+F4** to close the window.

The Least You Need to Know

Congratulations! You now have your Document Doctorate. Let's review what you learned:

☛ To open a new document window, click on the **New** button on the Toolbar or use the File **New** command.

☛ To open an existing document, click on the **Open** button on the Toolbar or use the **File Open** command.

☛ To return to the last editing place in a document, press **Shift+F5**.

☛ If you can't find a document, use the **Find File** command on the **File** menu or within the Open dialog box. You can find a file in many ways: by name, by contents, and by date, just to name a few.

☛ Once you've found a file or files, you can open them, copy them, print them, or delete them. You can also preview their contents or their document summary before using them.

continues

continued

☞ You can open up to nine documents at the same time. To move to another document window, open the **Window** menu and select the document you want. If more than one window is displayed on the screen, you can click on a window or press **Alt+F6** to make another window active.

☞ You can work on two sections of the same document by splitting the window into panes. Double-click on the split box or open the Control-menu box and select the **Split** command.

☞ To adjust the size of the two panes, drag the split bar, or press **Alt+–** (hyphen) to open the Control menu and select the **Split** command. Then use the arrow keys to adjust the size of the panes and press **Enter**. To return to one window, double-click on the split bar or use the **Split** command again to move the split bar off the window and press **Enter**.

☞ To move between the two panes, click inside a pane to make it active or press **F6** to toggle back and forth.

Chapter 9
Saving Your Docs for a Rainy Day

In This Chapter

☞ How to save a new document

☞ Valid names for your files

☞ Saving all your files with one step

☞ Creating a copy of a document

☞ Saving your documents automatically

☞ Closing document windows

Save a document, save a life. Okay, maybe it's not that dramatic, but by saving your documents often, you can save yourself a lot of time and trouble if something happens to your computer (such as a power failure).

If you don't want to bother with remembering to save files often, you can configure Word for Windows so it saves your files at regular intervals. If it makes things easier for your computer, you can also have Word keep track of all the changes you make to a document, and save just those changes at *periodic intervals*.

> ## By the Way . . .
>
> I like that term "periodic intervals," don't you? I try to use it often to make me sound smart: "In the morning, I need coffee at *periodic intervals*." Feel free to try it yourself: "Before I found this wonderful book to help me, I used to toss my computer against the wall at *periodic intervals*. Now I toss my computer manual."

When Should I Save a Document?

You'll always want to save your document prior to exiting Word for Windows (because otherwise, it's gonno!). But you may also want to save the document periodically during a long work session.

Any time is a great time to save your documents, but I like to save them just before I attempt some complicated task, and again when I finish that task correctly. I also save documents just prior to printing.

Knowing that you should save your documents frequently is one thing; remembering to do it is another. You can configure Word for Windows so that it periodically saves your work for you. Stay tuned; you'll learn how later in this chapter.

File   DOS stores information in files. Anything can be placed in a file: a memo, a budget report, or even a graphics image (like a picture of a boat or a computer). Each document you create in Word for Windows is stored in its own file.

A Document by Any Other File Name Would Still Spell As Sweet

Shakespeare would argue that there's not much in a file name, but I have to disagree. Naming your documents so you can identify them easily is an important timesaver when it comes time to locate them. DOS must agree with Shakespeare though, because it gives you very little room to be informative when naming your *files*.

Each file name has a first and a last name. The last name (called the *extension*) helps to identify the file's type. Word for Windows uses an extension of .DOC to identify your files as documents. You give your documents their first names, which can be as long as eight characters. Let me give you some examples:

93BUDGET.DOC

TO_DO.DOC

4THQTR.DOC

COVLETTR.DOC

WHATS_UP.DOC

RESUME.DOC

You can use letters and numbers, and even an underscore as a substitute space (you can't use actual spaces), but you can't go over eight characters. Don't worry about the extension; Word for Windows adds the .DOC extension for you.

Now that you know how to name your files, let's get down to the business of saving them.

What's Wrong with This Picture?

Joey wants to give his document a descriptive file name. The document is a sales report for the Northwest Region, so he types NORTHWEST.DOC. What's wrong with this picture?

Answer: Joey used too many letters; he can only use eight characters (excluding the three-character extension). Joey decides to call the file NW SALES.DOC instead. Now what's wrong with this picture?

Answer: Joey forgot that you can't use spaces in a file name. Joey can really use some help. Can you choose a valid file name from the list below?

NWSALESDOC

NW_SALES.DOC

N.W.SALES.DOC

Answer: NW_SALES.DOC is the only one that's valid. It has eight characters exactly (including the underscore). NWSALESDOC doesn't work
because Joey didn't put the period in before the .DOC extension, so
Word thinks that NWSALESDOC is the file name, and it's too long.
N.W.SALES.DOC doesn't work because you can only have one period in
a file name, and it goes right before the extension, as in .DOC.

There's a First Time for Everything: Saving a Document

Saving your document for the first time is a little bit more complex than
saving it later on, because you must answer some basic questions (such as
"What do you want to call this thing?") before Word can save your work.
Here's the play-by-play:

First, select **File** from the main menu and choose **Save**, or click on
the **Save** button on the Toolbar. Then type the name for your file.
Remember not to use more than eight characters. Also, you don't have to
add the .DOC extension but if you do, separate it from the file name with
a period, as in CH09.DOC.

Type a name for your file.

Change drives or directories.

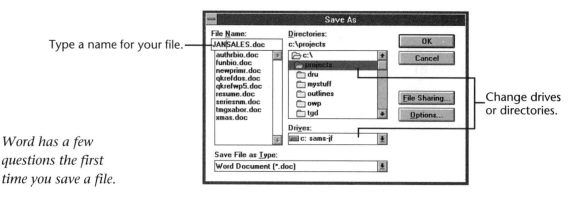

*Word has a few
questions the first
time you save a file.*

If you want to save your file in a different drive or directory, select a different disk drive from the drop-down list box. If you need to change to another directory, click on that directory, or press **Tab** until **Directories** is highlighted, and then use the down arrow key to select the directory.

If a file with the name you want to use already exists, Word will ask you if you want to replace the existing file. If you don't, type a different file name.

If you want to save the document for use with another program, you may want to change the file type. Select a file type from the Save File as Type drop-down list box.

To protect your document against changes, use the File Sharing button. You can make this document *password protected* (no one can open the document without the password of up to 15 characters), and/or *lock it for annotations only* (others can add sidenotes that don't print, but they can't change the text). You can learn more about annotations in Chapter 22.

By the Way . . .

Once you protect a document, no one but you can make changes to it. How does Word distinguish who you are? Well, when a document is saved, an author's name is inserted into the Summary Info box and stored with the file. When you open a protected file later, Word checks the name in the user information area against the summary information. You can change the name of the Word "user" by opening the Tools menu and selecting **Options**. Under **Category**, select **User Info** and then change the name and click on **OK**.

By the way, if you are the author of a document, you always have full access to it—so, if you want to "unprotect" the document later on, you have the right to do so. Just use the File Save **As** command, click on the **File Sharing** button, and change the option.

Whew. Now that you're done, press **Enter** or click on **OK**, and Word for Windows saves the document with the name you specified.

Entering the Summary Information

Before Word saves your document, it displays the Summary Info box. The information you enter here can be used to locate the document later. This information can also be included within the document itself, in order to print valuable details, such as the author's name and the working title. You can change this information later by using the Summary Info command on the File menu.

Summary Info	
File Name: JANSALES.DOC	OK
Directory: C:\PROJECTS\WWI\FIGS	Cancel
Title: January Sales Analysis	Statistics...
Subject:	
Author: Jennifer Flynn	
Keywords: sales, january, 1993	
Comments:	

Just a few questions, please.

Don't leave document windows open if you're done with them; they just add to screen clutter and make it more difficult to work. (I'm writing this as I search for a disk under tons of paper and other stuff on my desk. I thought you'd appreciate the irony.) If you continue working on your document after saving it, remember to save the file again before you exit.

After Word saves the file, it returns you to your document so you can keep on working. If you're done with the file, close it and start work on another file, or exit Word for Windows.

Saving It All

You can save all your open documents in one fell swoop by using the Save All command on the File menu. Using this command saves other files (such as customized dictionaries) as well.

Saving Once, Saving Twice

After a file has been saved for the first time, whenever you use the File Save command or the Save button, your document is simply saved to the disk with the same name you used when you first saved it. This process updates the existing file with the changes you've made.

What if you're creating a revision to a document, and you want to save this version under a new name? To save a document under a different file name, you need its birth certificate, Social Security card, several IRS tax forms, and the Save As command.

First, select File from the main menu, and choose the Save As command. If you want a quicker method, simply press **F12**, and a dialog box appears. (Do not use the Save button on the Toolbar, because it just saves the file without allowing you to make any changes.) Don't think you've gone crazy; this is the same box that appears when you first save a file. Why should Word use two boxes when one will do?

Next, type the new name for your file. Remember not to use more than eight characters. Also, you don't have to add the .DOC extension, but if you do, separate it from the file name with a period, as in CH09.DOC.

If you want to save this copy of your file in a different drive or directory, select a different disk drive from the Drives drop-down list box. If you need to change to another directory, click on that directory, or press **Tab** until **Directories** is highlighted, then use the down arrow key to select a directory.

Since this is the same dialog box, if you want to save this copy for use with another program or protect (or unprotect) your document against changes, follow the directions given earlier. When you're done, press **Enter** or click on **OK**, and Word for Windows saves the document with the name you specified.

You can make copies of several files at one time with the Find File command. Refer to Chapter 8 if you need a refresher.

Putting Word on Automatic

You won't have to worry when a storm shuts down your computer's power if you've saved your data recently. But if you're the kind of person who gets so involved in working that you forget to save, you may want to have Word save your changes automatically. Here's how you set it up.

Start out by opening the Tools menu and selecting the Options command. Then move to the Category column and select **Save**. If you're using a keyboard, press **Alt+C** and then use the arrow keys to move to Save.

Find the Automatic Save Every check box and click on it or press **Alt+S**. Type the number of minutes you want Word to wait between automatic saves. You can enter any number between 1 and 120, but I recommend 10 or 15 minutes. When you're through, click on the **OK** button.

There are some other options you might be interested in, such as Allow Fast Saves, which speeds up the saving process but costs memory and hard disk space that your computer may not have available. A check box that is already checked for you, Always Create Backup Copy, will save the previous version in a file with a .BAK extension every time you save.

Before closing a document, you should save it. When you exit Word for Windows, all files are automatically closed, so you should save your files before you quit.

Be careful not to double-click on the bigger square just above the document window Control-menu box; that will cause you to exit Word for Windows.

Closing a Document and Going Home

My mom was always yelling at us to close the door: "Do you think I want to heat the outside?" Along that same vein, you should close document windows after you're finished working with them. Of course, you probably won't have your mother to remind you, but remembering to close windows when you're through will eliminate clutter and make it easier for you to work.

To close the active document window, double-click on the Control-menu box (that's the square with a dash in it, in the upper left corner of the *document* window). If you are using a keyboard, press **Ctrl+F4** to close the active document window.

If you have more than one document open, the other windows will be unaffected by your actions.

The Least You Need to Know

As we bring this chapter to a "close," let's review what we've learned:

- ☞ Always save your documents before exiting Word for Windows, and before and after any complicated task. It's also a good idea to save your document prior to printing.

- ☞ File names consist of up to eight characters, with a three-character extension. Word for Windows documents use a .DOC extension, as in CH09.DOC.

- ☞ To save a document, click on the **Save** button on the Toolbar.

- ☞ You can save a copy of your current document under a new name with the Save **As** command on the **File** menu.

- ☞ To set up Word for Windows so it automatically saves documents, use the **O**ptions command on the **To**ols menu.

- ☞ You can close a document window after you've saved the file, and get it out of your way. To close a document window, double-click on the window's Control-menu box.

This page unintentionally left blank.

Chapter 10

Hold the Presses, It's Time to Print!

In This Chapter

- ☛ Printing your document
- ☛ Selecting certain pages or text to print
- ☛ Printing just the current page
- ☛ Printing multiple copies of a document
- ☛ Changing the orientation of the printed page
- ☛ Printing an envelope
- ☛ What to do when your printer is having a bad day
- ☛ Selecting the printer to use

There's nothing better than holding the result of your hard work in your own hands. After I've wrestled with Word for hours trying to get a document to look exactly the way I want, I get this overpowering feeling to jump up and say, "See? I did this!"

You might be experiencing something like this now, since your document is just about ready to print. In this chapter, you'll learn how to do just that, and if you experience any problems along the way, there's a troubleshooting section at the end of the chapter to help you out.

A Sneak Preview Is a Good Idea Before You Print

Before you print your document, you should look at it in Print Preview or Page Layout view. These two viewing modes show you what your document will look like when printed, so you can make sure that everything is the way you want it *before you print.* Print Preview displays a few more items than Page Layout view, but you can make only limited changes using it. So choose the viewing mode that best suits your needs. If you need a re-"view" of viewing modes, see Chapter 7.

The Printed Word

It's always a good idea to save a document before you print it, in case you run into printer errors or other problems. Click on the **Save** button on the Toolbar, or use the Save command on the File menu.

Printing the active document is easy if you want to print the entire document, and you want only one copy of it. Later in this chapter, you'll learn how you can be selective in what you're printing. But for now, let's start with the basics. First, repaginate the document so that the page numbers are accurate. When extensive changes are made, Word for Windows occasionally runs out of fingers and loses track of the real page numbers. Repaginating makes sure that the page numbers you might be printing at the top or bottom of each page are correct. To repaginate, open the Tools menu and select the Repaginate Now command.

To print a document with the mouse, just click on the **Print** button on the Toolbar. The active document will start printing according to the print defaults, which specify printing just one copy and printing the entire document. If you want to print more than one copy or less than the entire document, you'll need to use the File Print command described next.

To print the current document using the keyboard, select the Print command on the File menu by pressing **Alt+F** then **P**. When you use this command, a dialog box appears allowing you to change some of the print defaults, such as the number of copies you want. You'll learn what each of these options is for in later sections of this chapter, but if you just want to print one copy of the entire document, choose **OK** and that's it!

If you have problems printing, check out the troubleshooting section later in this chapter.

Printing Part of a Document

You can print only certain pages in a document if you want. For example, maybe one page was misprinted and you want to reprint it, or perhaps you need only one section of a complex document. Here's what to do.

Select the **Print** command from the File menu. (Do not use the Print button on the Toolbar; by default, it prints all the pages of a document.) Surprise! It's a box.

> If you need to stop the print job while Word for Windows is still processing it, press **Esc**. If the printer runs out of paper, a dialog box will appear telling you so. You'll be able to choose Retry or Cancel. Load more paper, then choose **Retry**.

```
┌─────────────────────────────────────────┐
│ ═ │            Print                     │
├─────────────────────────────────────────┤
│ Printer:  HP LaserJet IIP on LPT1:       │
│                                          │
│ Print:  [ Document        ±]  ┌────────┐ │
│                               │   OK   │ │
│ Copies: [1       ] ▲▼         └────────┘ │
│ ┌─Range──────────────┐        ┌────────┐ │
│ │ ○ All              │        │ Cancel │ │
│ │ ○ Current Page     │        └────────┘ │
│ │ ⊙ Pages            │        ┌────────┐ │
│ │    From: [2 ] To: [3]│      │ Setup... │ │
│ │                     │        └────────┘ │
│ │                     │        ┌────────┐ │
│ └─────────────────────┘        │Options..│ │
│                                └────────┘ │
│ ☐ Print to File      ⊠ Collate Copies    │
└─────────────────────────────────────────┘
```

You can print only part of a document if you want.

First, click on Pages or press **Alt+G**. Now you need to do some typing. Type the beginning page number in the From box, press **Tab**, and type the ending page number in the To box. When you're done, choose **OK**.

As an alternative, you can print the current page by choosing Current Page. You can print just the text you've selected by choosing Selection.

If you have a printer that allows you to select the number of copies to print on some kind of control panel, you may want to use that option instead of having Word print your copies for you. When Word prints multiple copies, it reprocesses the document over and over, using more time than your printer would to print the same number of copies.

I'll Take Two!

If you need more than one copy of your document, Word can print it for you and save you time standing in the copier line.

Start out by selecting the **Print** command from the File menu. Do not use the Print button on the Toolbar; by default, it prints all the pages of a document. When that dialog box appears, type the number of copies you want under Copies. If you're using the keyboard, press **Alt+C** to move to Copies and then type your number.

If you choose Collate Copies, Word for Windows not only slices and dices, but it collates, too, by printing all of one copy first and then all of the next. When you're completely finished, choose **OK**.

The Great American Landscape Mode

You can print your document in *portrait* mode or *landscape* mode.

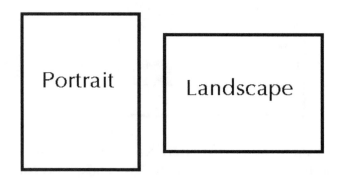

To change the orientation of pages within your document, just follow along with me.

First, open the Format menu and choose the Page Setup command. Then click on the Size and Orientation option button. If you're using a keyboard, press **Alt+S**.

Now it's time to pick a page orientation. Click on either the Portrait or the Landscape option button. If you're using a keyboard, press **Alt+R** or **Alt+L**. Select a portion of the document that this affects in the Apply To drop-down list box. You can choose from options such as Whole Document, Selected Text, and This Point Forward. For example, if you have a table on page two that you want to print in landscape mode, but you want the rest of the report printed in portrait mode, simply move the insertion point to page two and select **This Point Forward**. If your report has a page three, move to page three, switch back to portrait orientation, and again select **This Point Forward**. When you're finished, choose **OK**.

Portrait orientation
Your document is oriented so that it is longer than it is wide, as in 8 1/2" x 11". This is the normal orientation of most documents.

Landscape orientation Your document is oriented so that it is wider than it is long, as in 11" x 8 1/2".

The Envelope, Please

Word makes it incredibly easy to prepare an envelope for a letter. The only thing that you'll find hard about this is getting your printer to print the darn thing—so I'll give you some tips in a moment. First, the easy part.

Start out by selecting the address you want on the envelope. If you didn't include the address in your letter, that's okay—just skip this step.

 Click on the **Envelope** button on the Toolbar. If you don't use a mouse, select the Create Envelope command on the Tools menu. When the dialog box appears, if you didn't select an address earlier, you'll have to type one in the Addressed To box.

Next, enter your return address by clicking in the Return Address box or by pressing **Tab**. The first time you use this option, Word will prompt you to enter your address. From then on, it remembers. If you have special envelopes and you don't want to print a return address, then use the Omit Return Address check box. If you're using a keyboard, press **Alt+O** to check this box.

Finally, check the envelope size. Make sure that the correct size is selected in the Envelope Size box. To change sizes, click on the down arrow to open the list box, or press **Alt+S**. Select an envelope size by clicking on it or highlighting it with the arrow keys and pressing **Enter**.

You can print it now, or you can print it later. If you want to print the envelope now, use the **Print Envelope** button (if you're using a keyboard, press **Alt+P**). Use the Add To Document button to print the envelope later, at the same time you print the document. Click on the button or press **Alt+A** to add the envelope to the document.

Some Quick Tips for Printing Envelopes

If you have a laser printer:

☞ You pretty much need a special thing called an envelope feeder. If you don't have one, check your manual for instructions on how to feed an envelope in some kind of "straight through" path that bypasses the nasty twists and turns that your normal paper takes through your laser.

☞ Check your manual to see if the envelope is supposed to be inserted in the center of the feed slot or against one edge (lasers vary on how they want this done).

☞ Most important of all: don't skimp on quality. Buy envelopes that are made for a laser. Other envelopes practically melt from the heat and really gum up the works (if you don't mind the pun).

If you have a dot-matrix printer:

☞ Line up the left edge of the envelope against the left edge of the paper feed.

☞ Move the tractor feed so the top edge of the envelope is even with the print head. Word will move the envelope up about a half inch before it prints anything, so don't worry that your address will fall off the edge.

Printer Jams and Other Problems You Might Encounter

There is probably nothing more frustrating than coaxing a reluctant printer to spit out some text. After putting all your hard work into creat-ing the perfect report, the last thing you want to deal with is a problem printer. If you encounter problems, check the printer cables to be sure they're plugged in tight, and verify that the printer is on and on-line (look for a button labeled *on-line, ready,* or *select,* which controls this). Here are some other things to watch out for:

If you get a message from Word asking if you want to retry, examine the reason for the error. If the printer wasn't on, turn it on and then retry the print job. If the printer ran out of paper, replace it and retry. If the printer jammed, retry if you have a laser, but cancel if you have a dot-matrix. (A laser printer has a better memory than a dot-matrix and can pick up where it left off.)

If you get something to print, but it looks like the printer is on drugs, you may not have the printer set up for use with Windows. Or if you have more than one printer, you may have chosen the wrong printer for this document. An upcoming section talks about how to choose a printer.

Now, some specifics you can try depending on the type of printer you have.

If You Have a Laser Printer

Use the right paper and load it correctly. Use special laser paper (I recommend 20 lb. and not a cheaper type of paper). Laser paper has a texture that is easier for the laser printer to grab as it moves through the printer. Do not use stuff that isn't specifically designed for a laser printer; use *laser* labels, *laser* transparencies, etc. Colored paper is okay, but avoid papers with dusty surfaces.

Watch out for hot parts—
a laser printer is full of
them. Most are labeled with
warnings, but be safe: try
not to touch any part unless
absolutely necessary.

Laser printers usually will
only eject a page when that
page is full. (I wish someone
had told me that when I
first got my laser!)

When the paper gets jammed (stuck), remove it.
Pop it open and carefully remove the errant page
just as you would with a copier.

**My laser printer seems okay, but nothing is
coming out.** You may need to form-feed (eject) the
paper by taking the printer off-line (press the **On-
Line** button) and then press the **Form Feed** button.
Then press the **On-Line** button again to put the
printer back into service. This should get the paper
to come out.

If You Have a Dot-Matrix Printer

Use the right paper and load it correctly. Be sure
that the continuous feed paper (if you use it) is not
caught on anything, and that the perforation is
just barely above the print head when the printer is
turned on.

When the paper gets jammed (stuck), remove it. If you have a dot-
matrix printer, turn it off. Use the print knob to back the paper out. Avoid
the urge to rip the paper out. It'll tear and you'll spend the rest of the day
with a pair of tweezers trying to pick out the last remnants.

Everything is printing on one smeary line of ink. Your printer isn't
getting the order from the computer to advance the paper before it prints
the next line. You can fix this by flipping a small switch called a *DIP
switch*. The DIP switch is usually located in some "convenient location,"
such as the back of your printer, or even inside. Look in your manual for
the location of the DIP switches. Each switch has a particular purpose, and
the one you're interested in is called "LF after CR" or "Add linefeed" or
some such. Turn your printer off, flip the switch, and then turn the printer
on and try again.

**Everything is coming out double-spaced even though it's single-spaced
in Word for Windows.** This problem is the opposite of the single smeary
line of ink. Only this time, the computer is sending the order to advance
the paper, and the printer is adding its own advance. Locate the "LF after
CR" or "Add linefeed" DIP switch, turn your printer off, flip the switch,
and then try printing again.

Printers and the Wonderful World of Windows

All the printing for Word for Windows is actually handled by another Windows program, the Print Manager. When you installed Windows, you told the Print Manager what kind of printer you had. When you print a document in Word for Windows, it simply packages it up and sends it to the Print Manager, and the Print Manager sends it to your printer.

When you're printing a document within Word for Windows, and the Printing message disappears from the screen, your print job has been turned over to Print Manager. So if you have any further problems, you need to go there to handle them.

The Print Manager's best feature is that you can pretty much forget about it. Once a printer is set up for Windows, it's set up for all Windows-based programs, including Word for Windows. Print Manager also is adept at handling multiple print jobs, so you don't need to wait until a printer is done printing before you start working again or print another document.

Although this book is not about how to use Windows, it's kind of hard to avoid it since you're using a Windows program. Here are some quick steps for cancelling a print job within Print Manager. If you "don't do Windows," refer to Chapter 3 for help in deciphering these instructions.

From within Word for Windows, press **Ctrl+Esc** to bring up the Task List. Select **Print Manager**. While Print Manager still has print jobs waiting to print, its little tiny icon will appear at the bottom of your Windows desktop. So as an alternative to using the Task List, you can open Print Manager from your desktop. Double-click on that icon to open the Print Manager window just as you would any other window.

All the current print jobs will be displayed. If you want to start a print job over because the paper jammed or for some other reason, just highlight the job you want to cancel and then click on **Delete**.

You can do other fancy stuff while you're here, such as reordering the priority of print jobs (just drag the print job wherever you want it to be in the print queue) and temporarily stopping and resuming the printer (use the **Pause** and **Resume** buttons).

Print Manager starts itself when you print a document and closes itself when it's done printing. There's an exception to this, though. If you open the Print Manager window (by double-clicking on its minimized icon or by selecting it from the Task List) and then re-minimize it after the print jobs are completed, Print Manager will remain open and minimized until you close it or exit Windows. Why? Who knows. It's just one of those things.

Default printer   The printer that was set up when Windows was installed.

Minimize the Print Manager window when you're done (click on the **Minimize** button). If you close Print Manager, you'll cancel all of the jobs waiting to be printed.

Embarrassment of Riches: Choosing from Several Printers

If you're lucky enough to have a choice of printers to use, you should tell Word for Windows *when you start a new document* which printer you'll want to use later when you print. If you don't specify, Word will use the *default printer*.

To change the default printer that's used with Word for Windows, open the File menu and choose the Print Setup command. When the dialog box appears, click on a printer, or press **Alt+P** and then use the arrow keys to highlight one. Choose **OK** when you're done. If the printer you want to use is not listed, you will need to install the printer through the Windows Control Panel. Get someone to help you.

The Least You Need to Know

Getting your document to print can sometimes be pretty irritating, but the whole process will go a bit smoother if you remember these things:

- ☛ Before you print your document, you may want to view it first in either Page Layout or Print Preview mode.

- ☛ Also before you print, save your document by clicking on the **Save** button on the Toolbar.

- ☛ To print one copy of all pages of the document, click on the **Print** button on the Toolbar.

- ☛ Use the **Print** command on the **File** menu to print selected pages or text within a document.

- ☛ You can also use the **Print** command on the **File** menu to print multiple copies of your document.

- ☛ Use the Page Setup command on the Format menu to change between portrait and landscape orientation for all pages or selected pages of a document.

- ☛ Use the **Envelope** button on the Toolbar to prepare an envelope for your letter.

- ☛ If you want to cancel a print job or change the priority of a print job, use Print Manager to do it.

- ☛ If you have more than one printer available, select the printer to use with the **File Print Setup** command.

This page unintentionally left blank.

Part II
Document Makeovers

The irony about using makeup is that most women spend hours trying to look as if they haven't done anything at all. I think of formatting as "makeup" for a document, and in this section I'll show you how to apply it. And believe me, if you spend two hours formatting a document, someone will definitely notice.

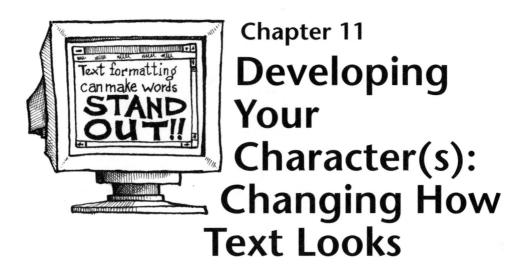

Chapter 11
Developing Your Character(s): Changing How Text Looks

In This Chapter

- ☞ Choosing the font (typeface) of text
- ☞ Quick ways to change the size of text
- ☞ Selecting various character formats, such as bold or underline
- ☞ Changing multiple formats at one time
- ☞ Copying character formatting to other text

Character formatting is the process of changing how text looks. For example, through character formatting you can make a word bold or underlined. You can also change the size of text (its *point size*) making it bigger or smaller. And you can change the style of text by choosing a different *font*.

Character formatting can be used to make titles, headings, and individual words stand out. Use character formatting to emphasize a point, create a mood, and visually organize your documents. (End of commercial; we now return you to our regularly scheduled chapter.)

Paragon font

Courier New

Paradise font

Mystical font

The font you select determines the mood of your document.

Font   Any set of characters that share the same *typeface* (style or design). Examples are Times Roman and Arial. Technically, font describes the combination of the typeface and the point size of a character, as in Times Roman 12-point, but many people use it to describe only a character's style or typeface.

Point size   The type size of a particular character. There are 72 points in an inch.

You can quickly remove all character formatting, such as bold or underline and even font and point size, by selecting the text and pressing **Ctrl+Spacebar**.

You can apply character formatting as you type a word or a heading, or you can go back later and select the text and change its formatting. I use both methods depending on my mood. If you change character formatting as you type, remember to turn it off when you finish typing the text you want to affect. (Think of it as a light switch; if you turn it on, you have to turn it off.) If you go back and select text, only the text you select is changed.

You can also use either the mouse or the keyboard to change character formatting. Again, I use a combination of both, depending on what I'm doing at the time.

If you want the formatting to apply to existing text, you first must select the text. Drag the mouse over the text to select it, or press and hold the **Shift** key as you use the arrow keys to highlight the text. Next, choose the formatting you want. More about this in a minute.

If you don't select text first, then the formatting you turn on will apply to the rest of the document until you turn it off. Turn off the text format by selecting it again; you can then continue typing.

Font Memories: Changing the Text Style

The type of font you use helps to set the style of your document: is it fun and light, or crisp and businesslike? One tip if you're new to fonts—don't overdo it (it's very easy, believe me). At most you may want to use only two or three font styles: one or two for different headings and one for text. Vary the size of text (point size) to create sections in your document, rather than choosing a different font (typeface).

By the Way . . .

If you have more than one printer, make sure you select the correct printer before you start working; the printer that's selected determines the fonts that Word for Windows makes available to you as you work. Change from printer to printer with the **File Print Setup** command.

Also, some fonts are displayed on-screen differently than when they are printed. So to be sure that you're getting what you want, use the **O**ptions command on the **Tools** menu. In the **Category** column, choose **View**. Then under Show Text with, toggle the **Line Breaks and Fonts as Printed** check box on and choose **OK**.

By the way, Windows comes with its own fonts, which it makes available to all Windows programs (including Word for Windows). These fonts are called TrueType fonts, and you can easily identify them because they have a little "TT" in front of their names. If you're trying to decide what font to use, use a TrueType font because TrueType fonts will print as you see them on the screen.

Remember that you can change the font and point size of text either before you enter it or after the fact by selecting the text and then following these steps:

Select a font from this box.

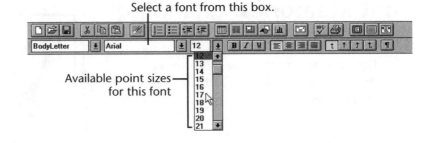

Available point sizes—
for this font

*Use the Ribbon to
change the font and
point size of text.*

When you remove all character formatting by pressing Ctrl+Spacebar, your text takes on the characteristics of the Normal style, which unless you've changed it, is Times Roman 10 point text. You'll learn more about styles in Chapter 14.

If you have a mouse, click on the arrow to the right of the font drop-down list box on the Ribbon to open it. Select a font by clicking on it. Change the point size in the same way: click on the arrow to the right of the point box and click on an available point size.

If you want to use your keyboard instead, press **Ctrl+F** to open the font box and use the arrow keys to highlight a font, and then press **Enter**. Press **Ctrl+P** to open the point box and follow the same basic procedure: use the arrow keys to highlight a point size and press **Enter**.

If you're typing text, remember to change the font and point size back to normal later on. Just repeat these steps again to change it back.

What's Wrong with This Picture?

If the Ribbon is not displayed, open the View menu and select Ribbon to display it.

Beth wanted to impress her boss with her department budget report, so she typed the upper report shown on the following page. What's wrong with it?

Department Budget Report

This month, we managed to take more calls, handle more special requests, and yet we didn't use a lot of overtime. I think you'll be pleased with the numbers: (see Attachment.)

As you can see, we did very well at increasing our volume while decreasing our costs. How did we do it? With the training I was able to provide my employees, they responded by handling calls faster and more efficiently. Jane, Pat, and Bill did an especially outstanding job.

How Can We Maintain This Trend?

I propose that we install a new telephone messaging system, such as the Caller 2000. This will allow me to direct the volume of calls to the fastest workers, increasing the chances of our clients reaching a representative. Also, with the Caller 2000, a customized message system will allow the caller to pick and choose from several options, so they reach the department they want with the least amount of hassle.

Department Budget Report

This month, we managed to take more calls, handle more special requests, and yet we didn't use a lot of overtime. I think you'll be pleased with the numbers (See Attachment.)

As you can see, we did very well at increasing our volume while decreasing our costs. How did we do it? With the training I was able to provide my employees, they responded by handling calls faster and more efficiently. Jane, Pat, and Bill did an especially outstanding job.

How Can We Maintain This Trend?

I propose that we install a new telephone messaging system, such as the Caller 2000. This will allow me to direct the volume of calls to the fastest workers, increasing the chances of our clients reaching a representative. Also, with the Caller 2000, a customized message system will allow the caller to pick and choose from several options, so they reach the department they want with the least amount of hassle.

Answer: If you said, "She's used too many fonts," you're right! Look at the lower report. This one uses only two fonts, one for the headings, one for the text. The size of the second heading is reduced to indicate that it's a subheading.

The Incredible Shrinking Text

You can increase or decrease the point size of text to the next available size by pressing these keys:

To make text one size bigger, press **Ctrl+F2.**

To make text one size smaller, press **Ctrl+Shift+F2.**

The amount of change will depend on the font you are using. Some fonts jump several points in size, such as 10, 12, 14, while others may go up one point at a time as in 10, 11, 12. It all depends on the font you're using.

Making a Bold Statement (or Italic, Underlined, Etc.)

There are many different kinds of character formatting:

Bold	*Italic*	~~Strikethrough~~
Hidden (not printed)	SMALL CAPS	ALL CAPS
Single (continuous) Underline		Word Underline
Double Underline	Super^{script}	Sub$_{script}$

For extra emphasis, you can "combine" any of these formats to create words that are bold and underlined, or italic double underlined, to name a few. However, Word supports only one kind of underline per character, so you can't have double word underline, for example.

Mouseketeers: How to Change Character Formatting

Because there are so many ways to select the character format you want, I thought it would be helpful to include the details in separate sections for keyboard and mouse. First, the mouse ways.

If you want to make something bold, underlined, or italic, just click on the appropriate button on the Ribbon. You can make text bold italic (for example) by clicking on both buttons.

Click here for bold.   Click here for underline.

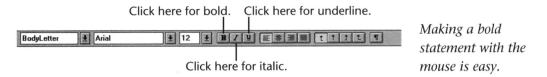

Click here for italic.

Making a bold statement with the mouse is easy.

If you want to make text anything else, such as strikethrough or double underline, you need to access the Character dialog box by double-clicking *between* any of the buttons on the Ribbon. This box also allows you to change the font and point size, among other things. It will be covered in detail later in this chapter.

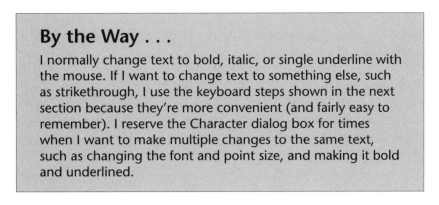

By the Way . . .

I normally change text to bold, italic, or single underline with the mouse. If I want to change text to something else, such as strikethrough, I use the keyboard steps shown in the next section because they're more convenient (and fairly easy to remember). I reserve the Character dialog box for times when I want to make multiple changes to the same text, such as changing the font and point size, and making it bold and underlined.

Keyboarders: How to Change Character Formatting

In addition to using the keyboard method for certain types of character formatting, I also use it when I'm changing one or two words in a sentence and don't want to take my fingers off the keyboard. Here are the key combinations for all the character formats:

To change characters to	Press
Bold	Ctrl+B
Italic	Ctrl+I
Single Underline	Ctrl+U
Word Underline	Ctrl+W
Double Underline	Ctrl+D
Small Caps	Ctrl+K
All Caps	Ctrl+A
Strikethrough	Ctrl+Shift+S
Hidden	Ctrl+H
Superscript	Ctrl+Shift+Plus Sign
Subscript	Ctrl+Equal Sign

Remember that you can select text first and then change it with these key combinations if you want to. If you use this method as you type, remember to press the same keys again to turn that character formatting off. Also, to apply combination character formats, such as bold italic, press **Ctrl+B** and then **Ctrl+I.**

To change capitalization, you can toggle through all caps, all lowercase, initial cap, and initial lowercase by selecting text and pressing **Shift+F3.** I use this when I type a heading too quickly and I've forgotten to capitalize everything, as it is in the heading below.

Put It to Work

Practice Making a Heading
Let's practice what we've learned so far about character formatting. Type something appropriately grand for a heading, such as "The Big Pompous Heading" or "Look, Here's Something You Don't Want to Miss."

Select the heading quickly by double-clicking in the selection bar (our invisible selection buddy that's located to the left of every paragraph).

 Let's start by making it bold. With the heading selected, click on the **Bold** button on the Ribbon or press **Ctrl+B**.

 Next, add single underline to our heading by clicking on the **Underline** button or pressing **Ctrl+U**.

Let's change the font by clicking on the Ribbon. If you have several choices, try a few of them out for fun. Next, change the point size of the text to something big. (Normal text is usually 10 point, so try 20 or something even larger.)

Hide and Seek: Using Hidden Text

Hidden text is kind of a neat option, so I thought I'd tell you more about it. To make some text hidden, select it and press **Ctrl+H**. Hidden text is displayed on your screen, but it's not printed when you print your document, at least not usually. . .

You control whether hidden text will be displayed on your screen with the **Options** command on the Tools menu. So if your text just went bye-bye (you can't see it on-screen), in the Category column, choose **View**. Then under Nonprinting Characters, toggle the Hidden Text check box on and choose **OK**.

Hidden text does not print, even if it's displayed on your screen. You can get hidden text to print if you need it to by once again choosing the **Options** command on the Tools menu. In the Category column, choose **Print**. Turn the Hidden Text option on, and choose **OK**. One warning: *displaying or printing* hidden text can throw off page numbering when you view or print your document, so keep that in mind when you use it.

Mix and Match: Selecting Multiple Formats at One Time

Whenever I want to make a lot of changes to some text, I use the Character dialog box. To get to this box, do one of these things:

If you have a mouse, double-click between any of the buttons on the Ribbon.

If you prefer the keyboard, open the Format menu by pressing **Alt+T**, then select the Character command.

Use the Character dialog box to select multiple formats.

This works like any other dialog box: click on items to choose them, or press **Alt** plus the underlined letter to move from place to place and use the arrow keys and the **Spacebar** to select items. As you make your selections, the Sample box shows you what your text is going to look like—which is a really nice feature in my opinion.

You can use the Character box to change the color of your text (the default color is black). Of course this works best if you have a printer that prints color; it's a nice feature to play around with if you do. You can still use color on-screen even if you don't have a color printer; this is a good way to display on your screen the editing changes made by someone else.

Put It to Work

Playing with That Heading Again
Select the heading you created earlier, and this time we'll use the Character dialog box to make additional changes.

Double-click between two buttons on the Ribbon or rub the lamp to make the Character genie appear. Let's change our underline type to double underline by selecting it from the **U**nderline drop-down list box.

Watch the Sample box change to see how your heading will look. Make some additional changes—have fun! If you don't want to keep them, click on **Cancel**; otherwise click on **OK**. The Character box makes it easy to change your mind, but it slows you down when you're making simple changes, like applying bold formatting. Pick the method that's right for you, or use them all like I do.

Mind If I Repeat Myself?

You can repeat the character formatting you just applied to another section of text by using the **Repeat Formatting** command. Select the text you want to copy the formatting to, or move the insertion point to a place where you want to type new text with this formatting. Then press **F4**.

If you're applying multiple formats, this method will work only if you used the Character dialog box instead of the Ribbon or the key combinations. If you did use the Ribbon or some key combinations to change character formatting, you can copy the formatting of text using this method instead: select the text you want to copy the formatting to, or move the insertion point to a place where you want to type new text with this formatting. Then move the mouse so it points to the text whose formatting you want to copy. Finally, hold down **Ctrl** and **Shift** and click the left mouse button.

The Least You Need to Know

All words and no character formatting make a document a pretty dull thing. Yours will sparkle with these tips:

- ☞ You can change character formatting either before you type or after you type (by selecting it).

- ☞ Use the Ribbon to change the font and point size quickly.

- ☞ To make text one size bigger, select it and press **Ctrl+F2**. To make it one size smaller, press **Ctrl+Shift+F2**.

- ☞ If you use a mouse, change text to bold, italic, or single underline by clicking on the appropriate button on the Ribbon.

- ☞ To change text with the keyboard, use the proper key combination—usually **Ctrl** plus some other letter, such as **B** for Bold.

- ☞ To select multiple formats at once, use the Character dialog box. To open the Character box with the mouse, double-click between any two buttons on the Ribbon. To open it with the keyboard, use the Forma**t C**haracter command.

- ☞ Repeat recent character formatting selections by pressing **F4**. Copy existing formatting by pressing **Ctrl+Shift** and clicking on the text whose formatting you wish to copy.

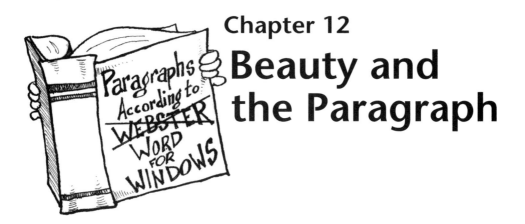

Chapter 12
Beauty and the Paragraph

In This Chapter

- ☛ The true meaning of the word paragraph
- ☛ Aligning paragraphs with the margins
- ☛ Changing a paragraph's indents
- ☛ Creating a hanging indent
- ☛ Changing the spacing before and after paragraphs
- ☛ Adjusting the amount of line spacing within paragraphs
- ☛ Copying paragraph formatting

You'll want to change the way paragraphs look for many reasons: to create centered headings, indented paragraphs, a right-aligned address, and bulleted or numbered lists. In this chapter, you'll learn how to turn your "beasts" into "beauties."

Webster's Gonna Get a Bit Confused by This

Here is the meaning of the word "paragraph" according to Webster's:

A subdivision of a written composition that consists of one or more sentences, deals with one point, or gives the words of one speaker.

Okay, now forget that definition. In Word for Windows, a paragraph is any collection of text or graphics that ends in a carriage return (Enter). This includes normal paragraphs, as well as single-line paragraphs, such as chapter titles, section headings, and captions for charts or other figures. When you press **Enter** in Word for Windows, you are marking the end of a paragraph.

You'll know paragraph marks are there when you accidentally delete one and the paragraph takes on the formatting of the paragraph following it. Turning on paragraph marks so you can see them prevents you from doing this.

So How Can I Tell Where Paragraphs Begin and End?

At the end of each paragraph, Word inserts a paragraph mark that is normally invisible, but that you can display if you want to. Why would you want to see these little paragraph "pests" all over your screen? To understand why, you need to know a bit about paragraph formatting.

Just as you can select characters and format them in a particular way, you can format paragraphs as well. For example, you can center a paragraph between the margins, change the indentation for the first line, or change the spacing between paragraphs, among other things. Paragraph formatting is stored in those paragraph marks that you don't see.

Also, when you press Enter to create a new paragraph, the formatting of that paragraph continues to the next one. This is kind of like character formatting. For example, if you turned bold on but never turned it off, all subsequent text would be bold. Once you make changes to a paragraph (such as changing its margin settings), those changes are effective forever until you change them again.

If the Ribbon is not displayed, open the **View** menu and select **Ribbon** to display it.

So to display these little creatures, click on the **Show/Hide Paragraph Mark** button on the Ribbon or press **Ctrl+Shift+8** (do not press the 8 on the numeric keypad—it won't work).

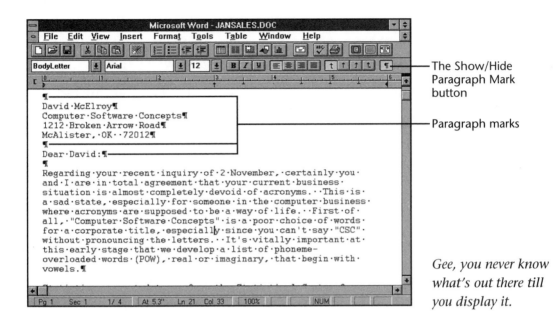

— The Show/Hide Paragraph Mark button

— Paragraph marks

Gee, you never know what's out there till you display it.

Some Things You Should Know Before We Go On

Before we get into actual paragraph formatting, I thought you'd like to know that the rules for character formatting apply here as well. You can format paragraphs as you type, or you can select them later and format them.

If you change paragraph formatting as you type (to create a heading, for example), you have to change it back later. (Think of it as a light switch: if you turn it on, you have to turn it off.) If you select already-typed paragraphs, only the selected paragraphs are changed.

In addition, you can use either the mouse or the keyboard to change text formatting. Again, I use a combination of both, depending on what I'm doing at the time.

If you want the formatting to apply to specific text, select the text first. Double-click in the selection bar in front of a paragraph to select it. Drag the mouse to select additional paragraphs. If you prefer the keyboard, press and hold the **Shift** key as you use the arrow keys to highlight the text. Then select the paragraph format. (We'll get to this in a minute.)

If you are using the method of selecting text and then applying the format, you're done. If you're formatting as you type, you'll need to turn off the formatting when you finish typing the text you want to affect. This is done by selecting different formatting. To go back to the original format, reset the formatting to whatever that was. Pressing **Alt+Shift+5** (on the numeric keypad, with Num Lock off) returns you to the Normal paragraph style.

If you need to remove a paragraph's *manual formatting*, select it and press **Ctrl+Q**. (Manual formatting is formatting that you apply yourself, as opposed to style formatting, which you'll learn about in Chapter 14.) When you press Ctrl+Q, you return a paragraph to its default formatting, which is determined by the style that has been assigned to it.

Okay, Everybody A-lign Up!

Paragraph alignment controls how the text in a paragraph is placed between the left and right margins. There are four types of alignment:

Left alignment causes all the text in a paragraph to line up evenly on the left-hand side. Text on the right-hand side is "ragged," which means that it doesn't form an even line down the page. This is the default paragraph style.

Right alignment causes all the text in a paragraph to line up evenly on the right-hand side. Text on the left-hand side is "ragged." This is the opposite of left alignment. I use this type of alignment to put a date or a return address in the upper right corner of my letters.

Center alignment causes all the text in a paragraph to remain an even distance between the left and right margins. I rarely use this for normal paragraphs, but I use it often for headings.

Justified alignment causes all the text in a paragraph to be evenly spaced out so that both the left and right margins maintain an even edge.

Depending on the size of the words within a single line, this can cause unequal spacing between words. This type of alignment is good for newspaper-style columns.

Changing Alignment

Here's what you do to change a paragraph's alignment. If you have a mouse, click on one of these buttons on the Ribbon:

 Left-Aligned Text button    Centered Text button

Right-Aligned Text button   Justified Text button

If you prefer to use the keyboard, use one of these key combinations:

Ctrl+L Left-aligned text

Ctrl+R Right-aligned text

Ctrl+E Centered text

Ctrl+J Justified text

Put It to Work

Playing with Paragraph Alignment
There's nothing better for learning something new than to play with it—work with it until it begins to make sense. So that's what we'll do. First, type in a sample paragraph that has at least two lines of text.

Use the preceding instructions to change its alignment to centered, left, right, and justified. In the next section you'll get a chance to practice indenting paragraphs, and you can come back here and compare what the two options do to a paragraph.

What's Wrong with This Picture?

Mike created two paragraphs like this:

```
             Let's Reach Our Customerrs

I propose that
```

As Mike was typing, he noticed the mistake in the title (the word Customers was misspelled Customerrs). From the letter I, Mike pressed the Backspace key to back up to the title, and he ended up with this:

```
Let's Reach Our CustomerrsI propose that
```

The question is this: what happened to the centering alignment of the title? Why did it become left-aligned?

Answer: When Mike noticed that the title was misspelled, he should have used the cursor to move back to the title. By using the Backspace key, he backed up and deleted the paragraph mark for the title. This deleted its formatting, so that the title took on the formatting of the paragraph following it (the title became left-aligned).

If the Ruler is not displayed, open the **View** menu and select **Ruler** to display it.

Indents: A Paragraph Margin's First Cousin

I think of indents as the first cousins to margins because they are so closely related (as a matter of fact, it's really easy to get the two mixed up). An *indent* is the amount of distance from the page margin to the edge of your paragraph. A *margin* is an invisible boundary that runs down both edges of the page. Normally, a paragraph flows between the margins, but an indent allows you to move the edges of individual paragraphs an extra distance away from (or toward) the margin. The easiest way to change indents is with the Ruler. You can set these indents:

First Line   Indents the first line of a paragraph the indicated distance from the left margin. You can even create a *hanging indent*.

Left   Indents all the lines of a paragraph the indicated distance from the left margin.

Right   Indents all the lines of a paragraph the indicated distance from the right margin.

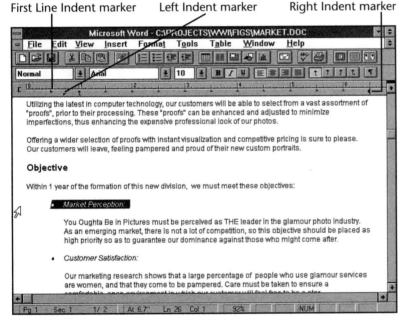

First Line Indent marker   Left Indent marker   Right Indent marker

Putting a 'dent in a paragraph.

Putting 'Dents in Your Paragraphs

To change the indents of a paragraph, move the insertion point to the paragraph. If you want to indent several paragraphs at once, select them first and then perform one of the following actions.

With the mouse, drag the Left, Right, and First Line Indent markers on the Ruler. To create a hanging indent, hold down **Shift** as you drag the First Line Indent marker to the left of the Left Indent marker.

If you prefer to use the keyboard, press **Ctrl+Shift+F10** to move to the Ruler. Use the arrow keys to move along the Ruler to the place where you want to set an indent. Then press L, R, or F to set the appropriate indent. Repeat all this stuff as needed to set the other indents.

If you want to move the left indent inside the left margin (to create a heading that starts inside the margin, for example), press and hold **Shift** as you drag the Left Indent marker or move the arrow keys.

You can quickly indent a paragraph one tab stop from the left by clicking on the **Indent** button on the Toolbar or by pressing **Ctrl+N**. Reverse this by clicking on the **Unindent** button on the Toolbar or by pressing **Ctrl+M**. To create a hanging indent, press **Ctrl+T**, and the left indent mark is moved one tab stop to the right. Press **Ctrl+G**, and the left indent mark is moved back one tab stop to the left.

Put It to Work

Hanging an Indent

Let's practice using the ruler to create a hanging indent and then just play around. First, type two paragraphs with at least two lines of text. You don't have to get fancy here—you can type garbage if you want, I won't tell.

Now click within the first paragraph to place the insertion point there. Hold down the **Shift** key as you drag the First Line Indent marker to the left of the Left Indent marker, and you've got yourself one beautiful hanging indent!

Notice how the changes you made do not affect the second paragraph, or the margin settings. What you're doing is adjusting the distance *between the margin settings and this paragraph*.

Drag the Right Indent marker and watch what happens. Play with all the indents to create different situations. If you want to try something really cool, create a one-line paragraph and pretend that it is a heading (you can even bold it or increase the point size if you want). Then press and hold the **Shift** key as you drag the Left Indent marker inside the left margin. This is a nice way to dress up reports, because the headings really stand out.

If you want to undo your changes to a paragraph, select the paragraph and press **Ctrl+Q**.

Hanging Around Numbered and Bulleted Lists

SPEAK LIKE A GEEK

Numbered or bulleted lists A special kind of paragraph with a hanging indent, where the number or bullet is placed to the left of all the other lines in the paragraph.

A special kind of hanging indent is a *numbered* or *bulleted* list. I've used bulleted lists throughout these chapters to

☛ Create snazzy lists like this one.

☛ Highlight what's coming up.

☛ Summarize the important points that were covered.

I usually use numbered lists when I want to explain the specific steps for doing something, such as step 1, step 2, and so on. Ready to number or bullet? Here's what to do.

 Click on the appropriate button on the Toolbar. Or if you want different bullets or numbering, use the **Bullets and Numbering** command on the **Tools** menu. You can change the type and size of bullets, the numbering system (letters, Roman numerals, or decimal numbers), and the amount of space between the number or bullet and the rest of the paragraph.

Spaced Out Paragraphs

You can adjust the line spacing within paragraphs (for example, making them double-spaced). A double-spaced printout is great for a reader who is also editing; it gives her space to write comments. Double-spacing was big with my high school English teacher—and boy did she use that space!

You can also adjust the number of lines (if any) that precede or follow a paragraph. Start by opening the Format menu and choosing **Paragraph**.

If one paragraph has spacing added after it, and the following paragraph has spacing added before it, the amount of spacing between the two paragraphs is the total of these two amounts.

Then, in the Spacing section, enter the number of lines to place before or after this paragraph. (One blank line after a paragraph is pretty normal, so why not try that?) If you set up a paragraph so that there is a blank line following it, you don't have to press Enter twice between paragraphs to create a blank line to separate them.

With the **Paragraph** command, you can also adjust the amount of space between lines in a paragraph. Under Line Spacing, select one of these options:

Auto	Lines are adjusted automatically to fit the point size of the font.
Single	Sets single space that Word can adjust as necessary.
1.5 Lines	Sets 1 1/2 line spacing that Word can adjust as necessary.
Double	Sets double-spacing that Word can adjust as necessary.
At Least	Sets a minimum spacing that Word can adjust as necessary.
Exactly	Sets an exact line spacing that Word cannot adjust.

If you're a keyboard user, press **Ctrl+1** for single spacing, **Ctrl+2** for double spacing, and **Ctrl+5** for 1 1/2 line spacing. You can also add one line of space before a paragraph by pressing **Ctrl+O**, or delete one line of space before a paragraph by pressing **Ctrl+0** (zero).

By the Way . . .

You can display the Paragraph dialog box quickly by double-clicking on any number on the Ruler. For example, try double-clicking on the number 2.

Mind If I Repeat Myself Again?

You can repeat the paragraph formatting with the **R**epeat Formatting command, just as you did with character formatting. Select the paragraph you want to copy the formatting to or move the insertion point to the place where you want to type new text with this formatting. Then press **F4**.

If you used the Ruler, the Toolbar, or the Ribbon to change the formatting of a paragraph, you should copy the formatting of the paragraph using this method instead: select the paragraph you want to copy the formatting to, or move the insertion point to a place where you want to type new text with this formatting. Move the mouse to the selection bar (the invisible area to the left of all paragraphs) for the paragraph whose formatting you want to copy. Then hold down **Ctrl+Shift** and click the left mouse button.

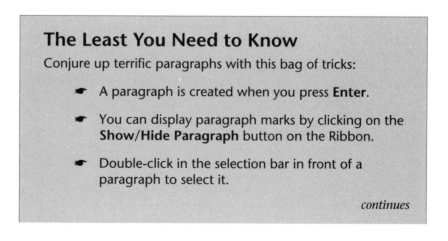

The Least You Need to Know

Conjure up terrific paragraphs with this bag of tricks:

- ☞ A paragraph is created when you press **Enter**.

- ☞ You can display paragraph marks by clicking on the **Show/Hide Paragraph** button on the Ribbon.

- ☞ Double-click in the selection bar in front of a paragraph to select it.

continues

continued

☛ Press **Alt+Shift+5** (on the numeric keypad with Num Lock off) to return a paragraph to Normal paragraph style. To remove manual formatting, press **Ctrl+Q**.

☛ Use the appropriate buttons on the Ruler to align a paragraph:

☰	Left	☰	Center
☰	Right	☰	Justify

☛ To change a paragraph's indents, drag the appropriate indent markers.

☛ To create a numbered list, click on this button on the Toolbar.

☛ To create a bulleted list, click on this button on the Toolbar.

☛ Change the spacing before, after, and within paragraphs with the **Paragraph** command on the Format menu.

☛ To repeat the last paragraph format, press **F4**.

☛ To copy a paragraph's formatting, select the paragraph to copy the formatting to, and then press and hold **Ctrl+Shift**. Click in the selection bar to the left of the paragraph whose formatting you wish to copy.

Chapter 13

Now You're Ready for the Big Time: Formatting a Document

In This Chapter

- ☞ Setting margins
- ☞ Adding a header or a footer
- ☞ Creating sections within your document
- ☞ Forcing a page break within a document

At last you're ready for the big time: formatting an entire document or simply *sections* of it. Formatting a document or a section is not as common as formatting characters or paragraphs—but the stuff you'll learn in this chapter will have a global, worldwide effect.

You're through with minor league stuff; here you get to play with the big boys. Let's start with the kinds of changes that affect an entire document—then I'll show you how to make these same kinds of changes for only part of your document (a *section* of your document).

Section A part of a document that has different settings from the main document for things, such as margins, paper size, headers, footers, columns, and page numbering. A section can be of any length: several pages, several paragraphs, or even a single line (such as a heading).

A Marginal Review

In Chapter 7, you learned how to change margins from the Print Preview window, so here I'll include just a quick review. To change the margins while in Print Preview, just drag the margin line to its new location.

When you change margins from the Print Preview window, you're changing them for the current section only. If you haven't created any sections in your document yet (hold on, you'll learn how to create sections in just a little bit), you'll change the margins for the entire document.

Pane What Word for Windows calls the special boxes that you use when adding headers, footers, footnotes, and annotations. A pane appears in the bottom half of the document window when you're in Normal View. (Since it's part of a window, instead of a separate box like a dialog box, it's called a pane.)

Headers Don't Have to Give You a Headache

A *header* is stuff that can be printed at the top of every page in a document, and a *footer* is stuff (such as page numbers, chapter numbers, and so on) that can be printed at the bottom of every page. You don't have to create headers and footers just to add the page number to every page in your document. Instead, you can open the Insert menu and select the Page Numbers command. Select either Top of Page or Bottom of Page. Choose the type of alignment (left, right, or centered) that you want, and then click on OK. Actually, the Page Numbers command places page numbers on all pages except page one. So if you want to place page numbers on every page, use headers and footers.

If you want to do anything other than just print numbers, such as adding text (for example, The Year in Review) or printing a date, use headers and footers. Headers and footers are pretty easy to create while in Normal view; you simply type text into a little box (called a *pane*), click on a few buttons to add page numbers and such, and you're through.

By the Way . . .

Word weirdness alert: you won't see your headers and footers in Normal view after you create them, so switch to either Print Preview or Page Layout view to see how they'll look when printed.

Here's how to enter a header or footer. First, switch to Normal view (open the View menu and select Normal). Then open the View menu again and select the Header/Footer command.

When the dialog box appears, choose **Header** or **Footer** and then select **OK** to open the box where you type in the header or footer text.

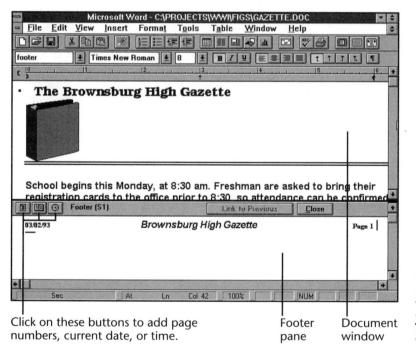

Click on these buttons to add page numbers, current date, or time.

Footer pane

Document window

When you create a header or a footer, you work in a pane like this.

You can also select special options, such as Different First **P**age (for a header that's different on the title page, for example) and **D**ifferent Odd and Even Pages (for headers that are different for the left- and right-hand pages). You can also change the placement of the header or footer in relation to the edge of the page if you want. In addition to all these choices, you can change the page numbering system (the default is regular numbers, such as 1, 2, 3) to other things like Roman numerals or letters, such as A, B, C.

After all the preparation, it's finally time to type the actual header or footer text. Press **Tab** one time to center text and twice to right-align text. Add character formatting, such as bold and italic, by clicking on the appropriate buttons on the Ribbon or pressing the key combinations you learned in Chapter 11.

Here's an extra nifty trick. You can add these fields to your footers or headers by clicking on the appropriate button:

Page number

Current date

Current time

When your header or footer masterpiece is complete, select **C**lose. Switch to Page Layout mode to see what the header or footer will look like (select **V**iew **P**age Layout). Scroll to the top or bottom of the page if you don't see your header or footer.

You can add headers and footers for each section of your document if you want; just repeat these steps for each section. Again, hold on because you're about to learn how to create sections in your document.

Slicing and Dicing Your Document into Sections

Well, finally I can show you how to create sections in your document. But in case you might be asking, "Why bother creating sections?," let me first give you some examples of when I've used sectioning:

☞ To create multiple chapters (for a book or a long report) in one document. Each chapter would have its own headers (such as the chapter title), and you could easily have Word generate a table of contents or an index for the whole document.

☞ For legal documents that require line numbering in some sections but not in others.

☞ To do a company newsletter with various formats. You could create a section just for the front page heading so that it reaches from margin to margin on a single line. Underneath, you could change to a three-newspaper-column format for the text of the newsletter.

☞ For business reports printed in portrait orientation (for example, 8 1/2" x 11") with a chart that's printed in landscape orientation (for example, 11" x 8 1/2").

☞ In a small manual where each section has its own page numbers. The Table of Contents section could use Roman numerals (i, ii, and so on) for page numbers. Each section after the Table of Contents could start with page 1. And since the title page wouldn't need a page number, you could suppress page numbering on just that page.

☞ To include text in two different languages (for example, a human resources memo). The document could be divided into paired sections—one section for English text and another for Spanish.

Time for a Section Break

Oops! Before I show you how to break your document into little sections, I should tell you this: set the most common document options first. For example, if you want most of the pages to have three newspaper columns, go ahead and set that option before you divide up your document.

Then when you're ready to start slicing and dicing, open the Insert menu and choose the **B**reak command. Under Section Break, choose from these options:

Next Page   The section starts at the top of the next page.

Continuous   The section starts right after the previous section, even if it's in the middle of a page.

Sections are marked by a double line in Normal view. Section marks are like paragraph marks; they contain the formatting for that section. So if you delete them, that section reverts to the formatting of the section before it. Just learn to ignore these lines; they won't print, and deleting them causes you to lose your formatting for your section.

Odd Page   The section starts on the next odd-numbered page. In a book like this one, that would be the next right-hand page.

Even Page   The section starts on the next even-numbered page. In a book like this one, that would be the next left-hand page.

Use the **OK** button to close the Section box, and you're done!

So Now That I Have a Section, What Do I Do with It?

Just look at the types of changes you can make that affect a section of a document rather than the document as a whole:

Margins   You learned how to change the margins of a document from the Print Preview window earlier in this chapter. If you decide to create different sections in your document, you can change the margins within each section separately—you'll learn to do this in a minute.

Paper size   You can choose from lots of paper sizes, such as 8 1/2" x 11" and 11" x 14", as you learned in Chapter 10. You can change the paper size by section, but this is pretty rare.

Headers and footers   A header is stuff that's printed at the top of a page, and a footer is stuff (such as page numbers, chapter numbers, and so on) printed at the bottom. You learned how to create headers and footers for an entire document earlier in this chapter. You can change headers and footers for each section of your document if you want, and you'll learn how in just a moment.

Page numbers   These are usually included as part of a header or footer. You can change the page numbering system from the default of 1, 2, 3 to something else, such as i, ii, iii or A, B, C. You can change the page numbering system within a document by creating sections and using different headers and footers for each section.

Newspaper-style columns You can create columns in your document that appear like those you'd find in a newspaper or a magazine (for newsletters and such). If you want to vary the number of columns to add interest, you must create a new section. You'll learn how to create newspaper-style columns in Chapter 20.

Breaking a Page Won't Break My Heart

One way to force Word to start another page is creating a section break and then selecting the Next Page option. But if you just want a page break, and no other changes, starting a new section is a little extreme. Instead, just use a forced page break.

I add a forced page break (called a *hard page break*) when I'm working in a section (like a chapter, for example) and I want to create a subdivision that starts at the top of a page. Maybe you want a supporting chart for a report to appear on a separate page. In any case, you can put a hard page break anywhere in your document by simply pressing **Ctrl+Enter**.

If you want to make one of these items different for part of your document (but not all of it), you must create a section first. For example, if you want to start your page with a large paragraph of text, then follow it with three newspaper-style columns, you must create a section. If you don't, the entire document will switch to the three-column style.

TECHNO NERD TEACHES

A soft page break (indicated by a dashed line) is one that Word naturally creates as text fills a page; it can't be removed. You can remove a hard page break, however, by selecting the break (indicated by a more solid line) and pressing **Delete**.

A Marginal Job of Sectioning

Earlier in this chapter, you learned how to change the margins for the entire document or for the current section of the document by using the Print Preview window. If you need to change margins for one or two sections, leave the Print Preview window and follow along with this procedure instead.

Facing pages   An option you can use when creating magazine-like reports; when open, the pages of your report would "face each other."

Gutter   The unused region of space that runs down the inside edges of facing pages of a document. It's the part of each page that's taken up when a book or a magazine is bound together.

First, select the Page Setup command from the Format menu. Choose the **Margins** option button and enter the margin measurements.

Two of these settings may confuse you at first. When you choose Facing Pages, everything does a quick switcheroo. What used to be the Left margin becomes the Inside margins for the report, and what used to be the Right margin becomes the Outside margins.

The Gutter is added to the Inside margin setting (or the Left margin setting if you don't select Facing Pages). You don't have to create a book to use Gutter; you could use the reserved space for hole punches if you're planning on putting your document in a binder. If you're having a professional printer produce and bind several copies of your document, you might want to leave at least half an inch of gutter space for them to cut the holes.

Next, in the Apply To box, select the area of the document you want those measurements to apply to. You can select Whole Document, Selected Text, This Section, Selected Sections, or This Point Forward. When you're done, click on the **OK** button.

A Footnote About Headers and Footers

Earlier in this chapter, you learned how to create headers and footers. If you want different headers and footers for parts of your document, read on:

- ☞ Create section breaks in your document with the **Insert Break** command.

- ☞ Move the insertion point so that it is within the new section and then use the **View Header/Footer** command.

☞ The options Different First **P**age and **D**ifferent Odd and Even pages refer to pages within a section. For example, the *first page* is not page one in your document, but page one *in that section*.

☞ You can also change the page numbering system within this section to make it different from other sections. For example, the front pages of most books (such as this one) are numbered with small Roman numerals, such as i, ii, and iii.

The Least You Need to Know

I hope that the last three chapters have left you with a feeling of total control: control over text, paragraphs, sections, and your entire document. (Now if I could only gain control over my waistline, I'd be a happy gal.) Here's what you learned in this chapter:

☞ You can change margins, paper size, headers, footers, page numbers, and the number of newspaper columns for individual portions of your document by creating sections.

☞ Create a section break with the **B**reak command on the **I**nsert menu.

☞ If you need to start a new page but not a new section, use a hard page break. Force a hard page break anywhere in a document by pressing **Ctrl+Enter**.

☞ You can change the margins for several sections at once by using the Page Setup command on the **F**ormat menu.

☞ To create a header or a footer, switch to Normal view and then use the **H**eader/Footer command on the **V**iew menu.

This page unintentionally left blank.

Chapter 14
Setting Your Own Style

In This Chapter

- What is a style?
- How to tell what style a paragraph is using
- Applying a style to a paragraph
- Copying a style from paragraph to paragraph
- Creating your own style
- Redefining a style
- Adding a style to a document template

After you've spent a long time getting a sidebar (for special notes), a heading, or a bulleted list just right (with special indentation, character formatting, or unique fonts), the last thing you need to do is repeat all those steps the next time you want to add another note, heading, or bulleted list elsewhere in your document. So what do you do?

You create three styles (one to remember each set of formatting selections), and you use those styles to create similar text in other parts of your document. And surprise, surprise, in this chapter you'll learn how.

Getting a Sense of Style

So what exactly is a style? A *style* is a collection of both character and paragraph formatting that defines a particular element *within a document*. For example, you can create a style for each different heading level within your document.

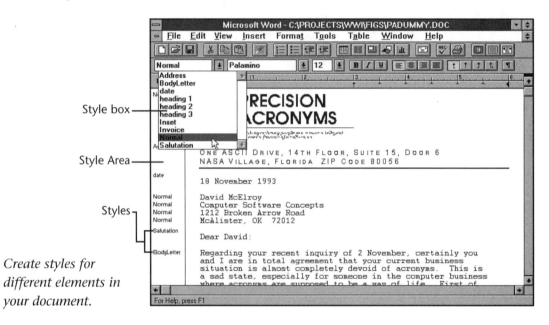

Style box ——

Style Area ——

Styles ——

Create styles for different elements in your document.

When you change the Normal style (its font for example), you're changing the starting point for all the other styles you create *in that document*. If you want to change the Normal style for all documents, there is a way to do that, and you'll learn how at the end of this chapter. Before you make any changes to the Normal style, be sure that's really what you want to do.

Now don't get too depressed; you don't have to create a style for every little thing. If a paragraph is unique, don't bother to create a style. But remember that styles save you the hassle of having to make the same character and paragraph formatting changes over and over again as you create your document.

Up until now, every paragraph you've typed has started its life in the Normal style: Times Roman 10-point font in a left-aligned paragraph. All other styles are based on the Normal style, so if you hate Times Roman font, modify the Normal style to use some other font before you create any new styles.

By the Way . . .

Ready to be confused? Don't read this unless you're really interested in how Normal style works.

When you make a change to your Normal style, whether or not the change affects another style in that document depends on what non-Normal attributes the other style has. For example, suppose you had a style called Title that was centered and 24-point and used the same font as Normal style (Times New Roman). If you changed the Normal style from 10-point to 12-point, you *would not affect* the Title style because its 24-point style is non-Normal—it overrides the Normal point size. If you changed Normal style to Palatino font, the font for the Title *would change* because its font (Times New Roman) is based on the Normal font.

When you create a style, formats that you change will no longer be affected by subsequent changes to the Normal style. Formats that you leave at Normal's default *will change* if you change the Normal style.

How Can I Tell What Style Is Applied to a Paragraph?

When the insertion point is placed in a paragraph, the style you are currently using appears in the Style box on the Ribbon. So you don't strain your neck looking up at the Style box all the time, you may want to show the paragraph styles next to each paragraph in your document. To do this, turn on the *Style Area*.

Style Area   An area that can be made to appear at the far left side of the screen, that displays the style for every paragraph in a document.

First, open the Tools menu and choose the Options command. In the Category column, select **View**, and then change the Style Area **W**idth to some positive number, such as .5 (half an inch). Choose **OK** when you're done.

The Style Area does more than save you neck strain—it saves you time selecting paragraphs and modifying styles. With the Style Area displayed, you can select a paragraph by clicking once on the paragraph's style name. If you double-click instead, you'll display the Style dialog box, where you can make changes to the style, assign a shortcut key for applying a style, or simply verify the formats that make up the style. Now that's stylin'!

Selecting a Style to Use

Let's start with simple things first. Suppose you wanted to section off text by preceding it with a heading. Well, you're in luck: Word has several heading styles already defined for you. Once a style has been created, all you need to do is apply one of the styles to a paragraph and make modifications if necessary.

Here's how to apply a sense of style. First, place the insertion point where you want the style applied. This can be an existing paragraph or some place within the document where you want the style to start. Select several paragraphs if you want to format multiple paragraphs at one time.

If the Ribbon is not displayed on your screen, open the **View** menu and select the **Ribbon** command.

Next, click on the down arrow next to the Style box on the Ribbon. Select an existing style. If you want to use the keyboard, press **Ctrl+S** to access the Style box, use the arrow keys to highlight a style, and then press **Enter**. To create a heading based on one of the existing styles, select heading 1, 2, or 3.

If you've assigned a shortcut key to a style, you can apply a style to a paragraph by pressing the shortcut key combination. (You'll learn how to assign shortcut keys later on in this chapter.)

Repeating the Same Ol' Style

To repeat a style you've applied to one paragraph for another paragraph in your document, select the same style again from the Ribbon.

If both paragraphs are visible on-screen, use this shortcut to copy the style. Select the paragraph you want to copy the formatting to. Then move the mouse to the selection bar (the invisible area in front of all paragraphs) for the paragraph whose formatting you want to copy. Hold down **Ctrl** and **Shift** and click the left mouse button.

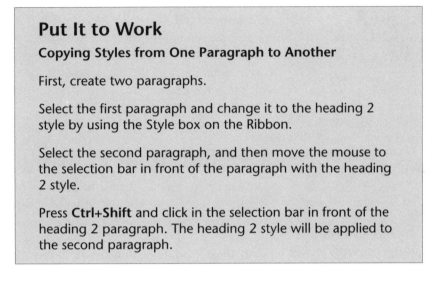

Put It to Work

Copying Styles from One Paragraph to Another

First, create two paragraphs.

Select the first paragraph and change it to the heading 2 style by using the Style box on the Ribbon.

Select the second paragraph, and then move the mouse to the selection bar in front of the paragraph with the heading 2 style.

Press **Ctrl+Shift** and click in the selection bar in front of the heading 2 paragraph. The heading 2 style will be applied to the second paragraph.

Creating Your Own Style

Let's create a style for the sidebar paragraph I mentioned earlier. Suppose you were going to use the sidebar paragraph for special instructions to the reader, and you'd like to add indentation, italicized text, and a different font to set it off from the rest of the document.

The easiest way to create a style is to format a paragraph first, and then use its formatting to define a style. So start by typing a paragraph that we can use as a sample. Then follow along with me to create your first style.

First, change the indentation of the sample paragraph to right-aligned by clicking on the **Right-Align** button on the Ribbon. Then select the text for the paragraph by double-clicking in the selection bar.

Next, make the text italic by clicking on the **Italic** button on the Ribbon. Finally, select a font from the Font box on the Ribbon.

When you create a style, it's available for that document only. If you want to make a style available for more documents (or if you want to make the changes to the Normal style affect more than one document), you must add that style to a template (which you'll learn how to do later in this chapter). A *template* defines the working environment for a document, such as its margin settings, page orientation, and so on. The template also controls which menu commands are available, and what tools appear on the Toolbar.

Word for Windows comes with additional templates that you can use to create specialized documents, or you can create your own. To see which template you are using, choose the **T**emplate... command on the **F**ile menu. If it says NORMAL under Attach **D**ocument To:, then you're using the default template. You'll learn more about templates in Chapter 18.

When you have the paragraph looking the way you want it, define a style based on it. With the paragraph selected, move to the **Style** box by clicking on it or by pressing **Alt+S**. Type a name (such as Sidebar) in the Style box on the Ribbon and press **Enter**. A style name can contain up to 24 characters, including spaces.

Redefining an Existing Style

If you want to change the font or some other characteristic of an existing style, it's pretty easy to do. Keep in mind that any changes you make to the Normal style affects *all other styles in this document*. So as a rule, you'll want to keep changes to the Normal style to a minimum. Changes to other styles are okay, though. Here's what you do.

Pick a paragraph that has the style you want to change. If you want to change the Sidebar style, for example, select a paragraph with that style. Go ahead and make any changes you want to the paragraph. Then select the paragraph again so that it's highlighted.

Select the style from the Style box on the Ribbon and press **Enter**. Word will ask you if you want to redefine the style. Click on the Yes button. If you decide not to change the style, click on the **N**o button.

What's Wrong with This Picture?

Mary decided that it would be good to create a style for a heading that she was planning to use several times within her document. She formatted the first heading as Palatino, 12-point, centered alignment.

After applying this same style to several headings within her document, she decided that she really liked the look of the Arial font. Because she wanted to use it throughout her document, she changed the Normal style to Arial. All of her paragraphs did not change to Arial. What did she do wrong?

If you accidentally changed a style and you didn't mean to, don't worry—just change it back!

Answer: If you guessed that some of her styles (such as the heading style she created) had been assigned a specific font, you're right. By assigning a font to a style (such as assigning the Palatino font to the heading style), she *overrode* the Normal style in the font category. So any further changes to the Normal style's font would be ignored.

Adding a Shortcut Key to a Style

If you want to add a shortcut key to a style, open the Format menu and select Style. From the Style Name list, choose the style you want to change. Under Shortcut key, select the Ctrl and/or Shift check boxes, and then enter a shortcut key letter (for example, you could use an S for the sidebar style). A message will appear if some other command is already using this shortcut sequence. If so, you should probably pick another letter, or deselect the Ctrl or Shift keys. Click on **Apply**.

To use the shortcut key, either select text that you want to change, or move to a place in your document where you want to begin using the style. Next, press the shortcut key sequence, for example **Ctrl+Shift+S**.

Saving Styles to Use in Other Documents

When you buy a VCR, chances are good that the remote that you use with your TV won't work with the VCR. After playing juggle-the-remotes for several years, I finally bought one of those universal remote things that works with both my TV and my VCR. Creating a style is like using the remote that comes with your TV: having the style is great, but you can only use it on that one document, unless . . .

Template   A template defines the working environment for a document, such as its margin settings, page orientation, and so on. A template also stores styles for you to reuse in every document that is based on that template.

Unless of course, you save your style to a *template*. Word has many templates already customized for creating common documents, such as memos, reports, and sales proposals. Word also has one central template called NORMAL.DOT, which is the template that all new documents are based on (unless you select some other template when you start a new document). So before you save your styles to a template, you'll want to see which template you're currently using by selecting the Template... command on the File menu. Adding styles to the NORMAL template makes those styles available to all documents; adding styles to another template makes those styles available to only the documents you create using that template.

Whew! If I haven't lost you and you're still interested in adding a style to the current template, here's how.

Start by opening the Format menu and selecting Style. Under Style Name, select the style you want to add to the template and click on the Define button. Then click on the Add To Template check box, followed by the Change button and the **Close** button.

When you exit Word for Windows, it will ask you if you want to save the global glossary and command changes. This is asking you if you want to save the changes you've made to your templates, among other things. Click on the **Yes** button to save the changes. If you decide not to save your changes, click on the **No** button; the styles you tried to add to the current template will still be available when you use the document.

The Least You Need to Know

The reason for creating styles is to save time in formatting paragraphs. This list will save you time in creating them:

☛ You can tell what style is applied to each paragraph by displaying the Style Area (select the **O**ptions command on the **T**ools menu). In the Category

column, choose **View** and then change the Style Area
Width setting.

☞ With the Style Area displayed, you can select a
paragraph by clicking on the style name. If you
double-click on a style name, the Style dialog box
will be displayed.

☞ To apply a style to a paragraph, select it from the
Style box on the Ribbon.

☞ To copy a paragraph's style to another paragraph,
select the paragraph you want to copy the style to.
Then press **Ctrl+Shift** and click in the selection bar
next to the styled paragraph.

☞ To create a style, format a paragraph and then select
it. Type a name for the style in the Style box on the
Ribbon and press **Enter**.

☞ To make changes to a style, change a paragraph with
that style, and then select it. Make sure that the style
name is correctly displayed in the Style box on the
Ribbon, then press **Enter**. Click on the **Yes** button to
confirm that you want to make changes to the style.

☞ To save a style to the current template, open the
Format menu and select Style. Under Style Name,
select the style you want to add to the template. Click
on **D**efine, check the Add To Template check box,
click on Change, and then click on **Close** to close the
dialog box.

This page unintentionally left blank.

Chapter 15
Picking Up the Tab for the Whole Table

In This Chapter

- ☞ When to use tabs, and when to use a table
- ☞ Setting tabs and adding tab leaders
- ☞ Creating tables and adding text to them
- ☞ Adding rows and columns to a table
- ☞ Creating a table heading

What is there to say about tabs or tables? Tabs and tables aren't nearly as interesting or as important a subject as global warming, the economy, Amy Fisher, or the clear version of Pepsi. I'm glad I don't have to write a whole book on tabs or tables (and I bet you're glad you don't have to read one). Oh, well, let's get on with it: to paraphrase the Latin poets of old, who never concerned themselves with tabs, tables, skin cancer, or Madonna's next album—"Carpe Diem!" Or more to the point, "Carpe Tabum!"

Picking Up the Tab

The Tab key in a word processor is like the Tab key on a typewriter. When you press it, the cursor jumps to the next tab stop (but it does not pass Go or collect $200). Tabs are great for creating short lists like this one:

Department	Department Number
Accounting	100
Sales	200
Marketing	210
Client Services	300

If you need more than three columns or more than just a few rows, you should probably create a table. A *table* makes it easier for you to enter large amounts of information, adjust column widths, and add borders and shading. You'll learn how to make tables later in this chapter.

Treatise on Tab Types

There are four different types of tabs, each one perfect for some suitable occasion:

Left-aligned This type of tab aligns characters on the left (the default tab type is left-aligned). For example:

Jane   Salesperson

Scott   Client Service Representative

Beth   Corporate Trainer

Right-aligned This type of tab aligns characters on the right. For example:

Description:

Syntax:

Example:

Decimal   This type of tab is great when working with numbers. It aligns numbers by the decimal point:

100.21

10.927

3515.65

.5586

Center   This type of tab is great for centering headings above your columns of data:

Stock	Buy/Sell
TM Technologies	Buy this one!
GSA	Sell right away!
American Paper	Buy this one soon!
Paramount Comm.	Buy lots of this!

Follow the Leader

Normally the space between tabbed columns is empty, like all the examples I've shown you so far. As an option, you can have Word fill the space with a *leader*. A leader is often used in a Table of Contents:

Introduction 1

Sales Analysis 5

Market Share 11

Fiscal Plan 13

The idea behind a leader is that it "leads the eye" across the page to the next item in the list. In this example, the leaders help you see that the Sales Analysis starts on page 5 of the report. There are different types of leaders: dotted, dashed, and solid.

Leader   Dots or dashes that fill the spaces between tab positions in a columnar list.

Take Me to Your Ruler: Setting Tab Stops

The easiest way to set tabs is with the Ribbon and the Ruler. Here's what you do. First, select the paragraph(s) whose tabs you wish to set. You can also pre-set tabs before you type if you want. Then click on the appropriate button on the Ribbon:

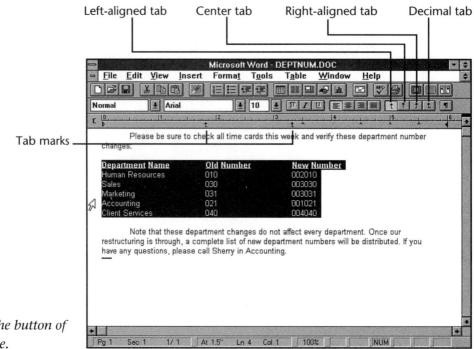

Left-aligned tab   Center tab   Right-aligned tab   Decimal tab

Tab marks

Click on the button of your choice.

If the Ribbon or Ruler is not displayed, open the **View** menu and select the appropriate command (**Ribbon** or **Ruler**).

Once the right button on the Ribbon is selected, click on the Ruler at the point where you want the tab to appear. Tab marks show up there in a shape that matches the button you picked on the Ribbon.

If you want to add a leader, double-click on a tab mark on the Ruler, and you'll see the Tabs dialog box. Click on the leader of your choice and then click on **OK**.

You can also use the Tabs dialog box to set precise tab locations. Again, either double-click on an existing tab or open the Format menu and select Tabs. Under Tab Stop Position, type a number to add a new tab. To delete an existing tab, select it and click on the Clear button or press **Ctrl+E**. You can clear all the tabs by clicking on Clear All or pressing **Alt+A**. When you're done, click on **OK**.

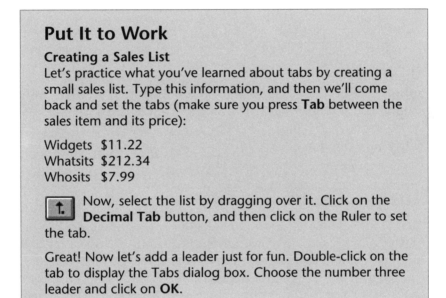

Getting Rid of a Tab

If you need to remove a tab, the easiest way is to just drag the tab off the Ruler with the mouse.

If you want to make this more difficult, do it with the keyboard. Press **Ctrl+Shift+F10** to make the Ruler active. Move to the tab with the arrow keys, and then press **Delete** to remove it.

What's Wrong with This Picture?

Look at this and tell me what, if anything, is wrong with this picture:

Salesperson	Territory	April Miles	April Expenses
John	North Canton	1230.5	1422.32
Georgia	Eastwood	933.12	533.76
Tom	South Canton	1221.6	1387.66
Laurie	Kints Cove	1330.56	433.89

Answer: If you said, "A lot!," you're right. First of all, leaders are not appropriate in this situation, but even if they were, leaders should not be used in column headings (the headings get confused with the data that way). Also, decimal tabs (and not left-aligned tabs) should have been used with the two numerical columns.

Setting a Table

A table makes it easy for you to keep food off your lap. In Word, it makes entering and organizing large amounts of information easier than if you use tabs. Tables are made up of rows (the horizontal axis) and columns (the vertical axis). The intersection of a row and a column is called a *cell*. If that sounds like the definition of a spreadsheet, you're right—tables are very much like simple spreadsheets.

By the Way . . .

You can use a table for more than just tabular data; tables are great for creating side-by-side text and/or graphics.

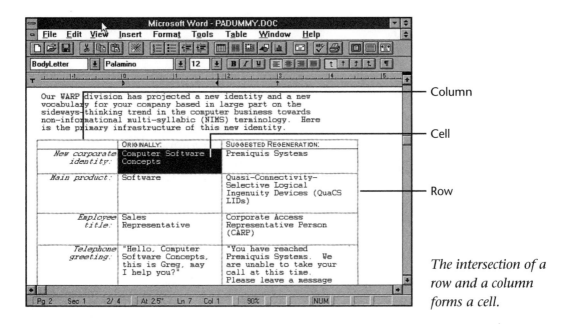

Labels on the image: Column, Cell, Row

The intersection of a row and a column forms a cell.

Get the knives and forks ready: here's how you "set" a table into your document. Start out by placing the insertion point where you want to set the table.

Click the **Table** button on the Toolbar and then drag over the grid to select the number of rows and columns. An empty table will appear at the insertion point with the number of rows and columns you specified.

The gridlines that you see help you enter data into the cells, but they don't print. You can remove them from your screen if they bother you by opening the Table menu and selecting Gridlines. When a check mark appears beside this command, gridlines are displayed. By selecting the command when a check mark is displayed, you toggle the Gridlines command off.

The Three T's: Typing Text in a Table

Enter text into a table by starting with the first cell. (If necessary, click in it to move the insertion point there.) To move to the next cell, press **Tab**. Press **Shift+Tab** to move to a previous cell. When you get to the end of a row, pressing **Tab** will move you to the first cell in the next row. Alternatively, you can click on a cell to move there.

If you use Shift+Tab to back up to a cell, the contents of the entire cell are selected, and if you type, you'll completely replace them. If you don't want to do that, use the mouse to click on a cell (this procedure does not select the entire contents of the cell). For you keyboarders out there, follow these steps: press **Shift+Tab** to move back to a previous cell, but before you start typing, use the arrow keys to move the cursor to the exact location within the cell where you want to add your new information.

Here are some tips for entering data into a table:

☛ If you want to type several paragraphs in the cell, press **Enter** at the end of each paragraph as you would at any other time. The height of the table will grow to accommodate the amount of text you enter.

☛ If you want to insert a tab in a cell (for example, you've typed several paragraphs in a cell and you want to indent them), press **Ctrl+Tab**. Just remember this: In a table, Tab moves you from cell to cell, and Ctrl+Tab moves you to the next tab stop. (Weird, I know.)

☛ If you want to change the width of a column, move the pointer to the column's right edge (the pointer will change to two vertical lines). Drag the column's edge to any location to make the column bigger or smaller.

Selecting the Cells You Want to Change

Instead of typing data, you can copy information from a spreadsheet program (such as Microsoft Excel) into Word, automatically creating a table. Use the old "cut and paste" method, with the Cut, **C**opy, and **P**aste commands on the **E**dit menu of each program.

You can select entire rows or columns in order to format them in one step. For example, you can select a row of column headings and format them as bold so they stand out. To select a cell or a row, just click to the left of it. To select a column, click at the top of it. To select an entire table, open the Table menu and choose Select Table or press **Alt+5** (on the numeric keypad with Num Lock off).

To select a single cell, simply press **Tab** or **Shift+Tab** to move to that cell. If you're already at the cell, you can press **Shift+End** to select the entire contents of the current cell.

Formatting Cells

After selecting the cell or cells that you want to format, follow the normal steps to apply character formatting. For example, if you want to make the selected cells bold, click on the **Bold** button on the Ribbon. If you want to change the font, select a new one from the Font box on the Ribbon. If you want to change the alignment, press the appropriate button on the Ribbon. See Chapters 11 and 12 for more tips on changing formatting.

Why do you have to add borders when they're already there? Well, the "borders" you're seeing are the gridlines that help you enter text into a table. Remember that gridlines don't print; to have borders, you must add them.

Another type of formatting that is especially effective with tables is borders (adding dark lines around cells) or shading (adding a bit of gray to darken a particular cell and call attention to it). See Chapter 21 for help with borders and shading.

Changing Your Mind: Copying, Moving, and Deleting Cells

You can copy or move the contents of cells by selecting cells and then clicking on the appropriate button:

Copy   Copy a cell

Cut and then Paste   Move a cell

To delete the contents of a cell, select the cell and press **Delete**.

When you *move* a cell's contents to another cell, anything currently in the cell you're moving to is wiped out (replaced). If you copy the contents of one cell to another, the contents of the second cell are placed at the end of the contents of the first.

You can move a cell's contents very quickly by selecting the cell and dragging it to its new location. To copy a cell, hold down the **Ctrl** key as you drag (if you don't press Ctrl, you'll move the cell's contents.) I find it easier to grab a cell if I position the pointer in the *middle of the cell* I want to copy or move, and *then drag*. When you move or copy a cell's contents like this, the mouse pointer changes to a small arrow on top of some little tiny pages. Look for this "flag" when you move or copy cells to let you know that "you've got 'em."

Put It to Work

Creating and Formatting a Practice Table

Click on the **Table** button on the Toolbar. Create a table that's three columns wide and four rows high. Type this information, remembering to press **Tab** to move from cell to cell:

Item	Regular Price	Sale Price
Widgets	12.00	11.20
Whatsits	9.75	8.15
Whosists	11.20	9.85

 Select the first row of the table by clicking to the left of the row. Then click on the **Center Alignment** button on the Ribbon to center the headings in their cells. Select the column of Items and center them as well by clicking on the **Center Alignment** button again.

Select row one again and click on the **Italic** button to make the headings stand out:

Item	*Regular Price*	*Sale Price*
Widgets	12.00	11.20
Whatsits	9.75	8.15
Whosists	11.20	9.85

 Now let's get those numbers lined up. Drag over the first column of numbers to select them. If necessary, change the scale on the Ruler by clicking on the [until you see a small T. Click on the **Decimal Tab** button on the Ribbon and then click on the Ruler to place the decimal tab. Repeat this process for the second column of numbers.

Item	Regular Price	Sale Price
Widgets	12.00	11.20
Whatsits	9.75	8.15
Whosists	11.20	9.85

Making Your Table Bigger

Want a bigger table? Just add more rows or columns.

To add more rows, select the row above where you want to add the additional row. If you want to add more than one row, select several rows. Then open the Table menu and select the Insert Rows command. New rows are added above the rows you selected.

To add more columns, select the column to the right of where you want to add the additional column. If you want to add more than one column, select several columns. Open the Table menu and select the Insert Columns command. New columns are added to the left of the columns you selected.

OOPS!

Why don't you need to insert a tab (by pressing Ctrl+Tab) in front of the numbers so you can later use the Decimal Tab button to align them? How can the Decimal Tab button align something that doesn't have tabs in front of it? Who knows—it's just another Word weirdness. Use **Ctrl+Tab** to insert tabs when you want to align text, not numbers. (I found this out the hard way, and I thought I'd pass it along.)

Put It to Work

Adding a Table Heading
Insert a row at the top of the table you created earlier in this chapter by selecting the first row of the table, opening the Table menu, and selecting Insert Rows.

Now we're going to merge the three cells in this row to form a single cell that we can use as a table heading. Select the new row and open the Table menu. Select the **Merge Cells** command.

continues

continued

Type this heading:

April Sales Campaign

Use the **Center Alignment** and **Bold** buttons on the Ribbon to center and bold the heading, and your table looks like this:

April Sales Campaign

Item	*Regular Price*	*Sale Price*
Widgets	12.00	11.20
Whatsits	9.75	8.15
Whosists	11.20	9.85

Spaced Out

Is everything all scrunched up? You can add more space between rows in a table to make them easier to read. Just select the rows you want to affect, and then open the Format menu. Choose the **P**aragraph command, enter the number of lines of space to add in the Before or After boxes, and select **OK**.

Remember that you can also add borders and shading to cells to emphasize important information. As a suggestion, you can add shading to every other row to make it easier to read across your table, instead of adding space. You'll learn how to add borders and shading in Chapter 21.

The Least You Need to Know

I'll put my cards on the table—here's what I feel were the most important points of this chapter:

- ☞ You can organize small amounts of information in columns by using tabs.

- ☞ There are four different kinds of tabs you can use: left-aligned, centered, right-aligned, and decimal. Each one is represented by a button on the Ribbon.

☛ To set tabs, select the paragraph first and then click on the appropriate tab button on the Ribbon. Next, click on the Ruler to set the tab's position.

☛ You can add a tab leader, which replaces the empty space normally taken up by a tab with dots or dashes. Double-click on a tab stop on the Ruler, and a box will appear enabling you to select a leader character.

☛ Tables are better to use than tabs if you have large amounts of data to organize. To create a table, click on the **Table** button on the Toolbar and drag over the grid to select the number of columns and rows.

☛ Enter data into the various cells in a table by pressing **Tab** and **Shift+Tab** to move from cell to cell.

☛ To change the width of a column, drag the column's right edge to its new location.

☛ If you need to move a cell's contents, select the cell's contents by clicking in the middle of the cell. Then drag the cell to its new location. To copy a cell, hold down the **Ctrl** key as you drag.

☛ To add more rows or columns, select the area where you want the new row or column placed, then choose either the Insert **C**olumn or Insert **R**ow command from the Table menu.

☛ To add a heading to a table, merge cells across the width of a table by using the **M**erge Cells command on the Table menu.

☛ You can add more space between the rows of a table by using the **P**aragraph command on the Format menu.

This page unintentionally left blank.

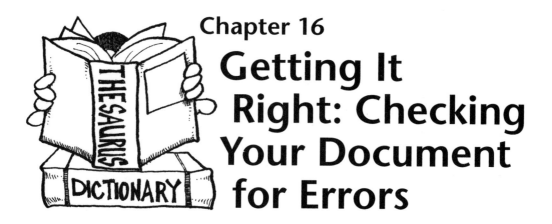

Chapter 16

Getting It Right: Checking Your Document for Errors

In This Chapter

- Checking your document for spelling errors
- Looking up an alternative for a word
- Finding grammatical errors
- Searching and replacing words within a document

I am not the world's best speller. Poor Miss Dingerham, she tried so hard, but I just never got it: "I before E . . . except in the 2,000 other words where it's E before I." Thank goodness for spell checkers, grammar checkers, and all those nifty programs built into Word that help me focus on what I'm trying to say, rather than how I'm saying it.

Spelling Bee

When Word checks a document for spelling errors, it searches for mistakes everywhere (it reminds me of ol' Miss Dingerham). Word checks headers, footers, footnotes, and annotations (but not hidden text). Spell checking a document is simple—just click on the **Spelling** button on the Toolbar. Word immediately starts checking for spelling errors. Also, if you've accidentally repeated a word, Word will tell you so.

For you keyboard users out there, follow these steps to spell check your document: first, open the Tools menu. Then select the Spelling command, and away it goes!

When Word checks your document for spelling errors, it begins its search at the insertion point. (You remember the insertion point: it's that blinking vertical line that marks your place in your document.) If you start spell checking from the *middle* of a document, at some time a message box will appear asking you if you want to spell check the beginning part of the document. Just choose Yes to continue.

You can quickly check a single paragraph or section of your document by selecting it first, and then clicking on the **Spelling** button on the Toolbar or using the Spelling command on the Tools menu. Only the highlighted text will be checked.

What to Do If Word Finds a Mistake

If Word finds a misspelled or repeated word, a box with more buttons than an airplane cockpit appears, giving you lots of options.

If you want Word to spell check your document from the beginning instead of looping around, move to the top of the document by pressing **Ctrl+Home**. Then start spell checking by clicking on the **Spelling** button on the Toolbar, or by using the Spelling command on the Tools menu.

If you want to spell check a single word, make sure that the insertion point is in the word and then press **F7**.

All these buttons in this dialog box and they still forgot one: Panic.

Spelling: English (US)
Not in Dictionary: veify
Change To: verify
Suggestions: verify / deify
Ignore   Ignore All
Change   Change All
Add   Undo Last
Suggest   Cancel
Add Words To: CUSTOM.DIC   Options...

Correct the spelling of the word. If you agree with the suggestion in the Change To box, just click on the Change button. If you want, you can type your own correction or select an alternative from the Suggestions list box.

If you want to correct this word throughout the document, click on Change All instead.

Ignore the correction. If you want to skip just this occurrence of the unrecognized word, click on the Ignore button. To skip all occurrences of the unrecognized word, click on the Ignore All button.

Add this word to the dictionary. That way, it won't be considered misspelled ever again. Just click on the Add button. Choose this option for specialized words that you use in your job, such as "cardiopulmonary," "electrolyte," "anthropomorphic," "Nanotechnology," or "Toolbar."

You can spell check a document by pressing **F7**. Normally, F7 is used to spell check a word or a selection, but after that's done, Word will ask you if you want to spell check the rest of the document. Click on **Yes**, and the spell check will continue.

Delete the repeated word. If a word is repeated twice and it shouldn't be, click on the Delete button. (You won't see this button unless Word encounters a repeated word.)

Undo a previous correction. You can undo any of the last five corrections in your document by clicking on Undo Last. This is great for people like me who love to click on the Change button, only to realize that the last word was spelled correctly in the first place.

You continue this process until the spell check is finished.

Handling the Informant

I was going to use the title "Using the Thesaurus" for this section. But then I decided to see what synonyms the Thesaurus would use to spice up my title. "Handling the Informant" is what it came up with. I guess that shows one of my reservations about using a thesaurus: it can make your writing sound stilted and fake. I mean, how often does someone say, "Our sales for the fourth quarter were consequential" instead of simply, "Our sales for the fourth quarter were great."

To use the Thesaurus, just follow these *consequential* (or great, important, considerable, critical) steps. First, select the word you want to look
up, or move the insertion point to the word. Then open the Tools menu
and select the **Thesaurus** command. A box "full of meaning" will appear.
The word you selected in the document appears under Synonyms For.

*You can select from
the alternative
meanings listed in the
Thesaurus box.*

Thesaurus: English (US)		
Synonyms For:	**Replace With:**	Look Up
affect	influence	Replace
Meanings:	**Synonyms:**	Cancel
influence (verb)	influence	
impress (verb)	change	
pretend (verb)	modify	
Antonyms	concern	
	sway	
	get	
	alter	

In the Thesaurus dialog box, you can select from several options:

☞ Choose from the synonyms listed in the **Synonyms** box.

☞ To change the synonyms listed, choose from general variations of the
   selected word in the **Meanings** box. If the Related Words or Antonyms
   option is displayed, select it to display additional choices.

☞ Look up additional meanings for the word displayed in the **Replace
   With** box by clicking on **Look Up**.

☞ Decide whether to replace the selected word. Click on the **Replace**
   button to substitute the selected word with the word displayed in the
   Replace With box, or click on **Cancel**.

The **G**rammar command is
just like the spelling checker
in that it starts checking
your document at the
insertion point. If you want
to start checking the
grammar at the beginning
of your document, press
Ctrl+Home. Then use the
Grammar command on the
Tools menu.

I Doesn't Need No Grammar Checker!

The Grammar command checks your document for
problems of a grammatical nature and makes
suggestions for ways to improve your writing and
clarify your meaning. As an added bonus, while
Word is checking your grammar, it also checks for
spelling errors.

To check the grammar in your document, open the Tools menu and choose Grammar. If Word finds something questionable, you see a box offering some suggestions.

Grammar: English (US)

Sentence:

Once our restructuring is through, a complete list of new department numbers **will be distributed**.

Suggestions:

This main clause may contain a verb in the passive voice.

[Ignore] [Change] [Next Sentence] [Ignore Rule] [Cancel] [Explain...] [Options...]

May I make a suggestion?

From here, you have these options:

☞ Accept a suggestion by selecting one of those listed in the Suggestions box and clicking on Change.

☞ Get more information about what's wrong by clicking on the Explain button.

☞ Make your own correction by clicking inside the document window and changing your text. To check the grammar in the rest of the document, click on Start.

Is the **G**rammar command being too picky? Or not picky enough? By clicking on the **O**ptions button, you can choose from predefined grammar styles, including Business or Casual Writing if you want.

☞ Bypass the suggestion by clicking on the **I**gnore button. You can bypass the entire sentence by clicking on the Next Sentence button instead. You can tell Word to ignore this "grammatical faux pas" for the rest of the document by clicking on Ignore **R**ule.

At the end of the grammar check, Word displays something it calls Readability Statistics: the total number of words, the percent of sentences that use *passive voice*, and the *readability index*. You can choose not to display this information by clearing the Show Readability Statistics After Proofing check box. For an average reader, look for a Flesch Reading Ease

SPEAK LIKE A GEEK

Passive voice   A way of saying things that shows what is done to the subject rather than what the subject does (for example, "The race was won by Mary Ann"). Active voice (as in, "Mary Ann won the race") is the opposite of passive voice.

Readability index   A measure of the education level a reader would need to easily understand the text in a given document. It is determined by counting the average number of words per sentence and the average number of syllables per 100 words. (A good average is about 17 words per sentence and 147 syllables per 100 words.)

of about 60, a Flesch Grade Level of about 7, a Flesch-Kincaid level of about 8, and a Gunning Fog Index of about 10. Numbers above these indicate some rather difficult material. (Translation: try this instead of two sleeping pills.) Numbers below these indicate easier material.

What's Wrong with This Picture?

After spell checking her document, Joan found this mistake:

> For the poor performance of our product, their seems to be no excuse.

What's wrong with this picture?

Answer: If you said that everything in the sentence is spelled correctly, you are right. Spelling is not what is wrong here; grammar is. Where Joan used the "their," she should have used "there." Would the Grammar command catch such a mistake? Try it and see.

Indiana Flynn and the Hunt for the Great Lost Word

Suppose you just finished a big report, only to find out that your client's real name is *Pets Are Us Incorporated*, not *Bill's Pet Shop*. You can use Word's Find and Replace feature to replace all occurrences of the incorrect name right before the meeting with the Top Dog. You can also search for a word without replacing it; this is helpful when locating the correct section within a document.

The Hunt Is On!

To find a word or a phrase in your document, open the Edit menu and select the Find command. Type the word (or phrase) you're looking for in the Find What text box. There are some handy options you can choose from:

☞ If you want to locate only the word you typed and not compound words (for example, you want to find "search" but not "searching"), use the Match Whole Word Only check box.

☞ If you want to match upper- or lowercase (for example, "Word" but not "word"), then use the Match Case check box.

☞ If you want to search backwards through the document, select the Up option.

☞ If you want to search for a word with particular formatting, use the Character, Paragraph, or Style buttons and make the selections you want. Click on **OK**, and you'll return to the Find dialog box.

When you have selected all the options you want, click on Find Next. Word begins the search from the current location in the document, but you can continue the search at the beginning by clicking on Yes when the message appears.

Word will look for the first occurrence of the selected word. If you want it to continue looking, click on the Find Next button. To return to your document, click on **Cancel**. To continue the search (search for the same text or formatting) at a later time or in another document, press **Shift+F4**.

The Great Switcheroo: Finding a Word and Replacing It with Something Else

To search for a word or phrase and replace it with other text, start by opening the Edit menu and selecting the Replace command. Type the word (or phrase) you're looking for in the Find What text box, and type the word (or phrase) you want to replace it with in the Replace With box. Here are some handy options you can choose from:

☛ If you want to locate only the word you typed and not compound words (for example, you want to find "search" but not "searching"), use the Match **W**hole Word Only check box.

☛ If you want to match upper- or lowercase (for example "Word" but not "word"), use the Match **C**ase check box.

☛ If you want to search for a word with particular formatting, use the **C**haracter, **P**aragraph, or **S**tyle buttons and make the selections you want. Click on **OK** to return to the Replace dialog box.

When you're ready to start, click on either Find Next (confirm changes before replacing) or Replace All (do not confirm). Word will look for the first occurrence of the selected word. If you chose Find Next, confirm the replacement by clicking on **R**eplace or continue searching by clicking on Find Next.

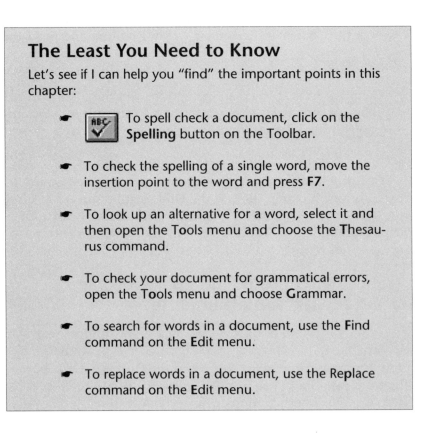

The Least You Need to Know

Let's see if I can help you "find" the important points in this chapter:

☛ To spell check a document, click on the **Spelling** button on the Toolbar.

☛ To check the spelling of a single word, move the insertion point to the word and press **F7**.

☛ To look up an alternative for a word, select it and then open the **Tools** menu and choose the **Thesaurus** command.

☛ To check your document for grammatical errors, open the **Tools** menu and choose **Grammar**.

☛ To search for words in a document, use the **Find** command on the **Edit** menu.

☛ To replace words in a document, use the Replace command on the **Edit** menu.

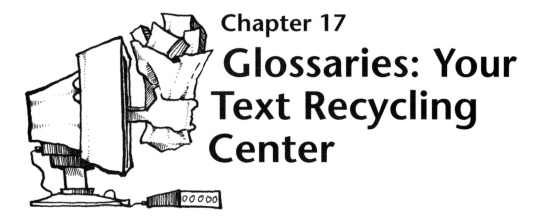

Chapter 17

Glossaries: Your Text Recycling Center

In This Chapter

- ☞ Recycling often-used text and graphics
- ☞ Creating glossary entries
- ☞ Inserting a glossary entry into a document
- ☞ Changing or deleting glossary entries

Recycling is a big thing nowadays, so it seems natural that even computers are getting into the act. Word for Windows comes with a word recycler called the *Glossary*. With the Glossary, you can recycle great phrases, such as "Ask not what your country can do for you," "Read my lips," and "It's a terrible thing to waste one's mind."

Glossary   A place within Word for Windows where you can store commonly used text and graphics. Using the Glossary saves you the trouble of typing repetitious phrases (such as a greeting and salutation) in every document.

Glossing Over Glossaries

Using the Glossary saves you the trouble of typing repetitious phrases (such as a greeting and salutation) in every document.

You can use the Glossary to store such things as

☞ A common greeting or closing for a letter.

☞ A distribution list.

☞ Your company logo.

☞ Your return address.

☞ Commonly used phrases, such as "If you have any questions, please feel free to call (someone else)."

☞ Instructions you often repeat, such as "Complete this form and drop it in the box outside of Human Resources" or "In case of non-compliance, sue."

Glossary entries are saved in the current template. The *template* defines the working environment, such as margin settings, page orientation, and so on. Word for Windows comes with additional templates that you can use to create specialized documents, and if you are using one of these templates, your glossary entry will be saved there. You'll learn more about templates in Chapter 18.

To make a glossary entry universally available, save it to the Normal template, because all other templates are based on the Normal template. (If you need to check which template you're using, select the Template... command on the File menu.)

Word Recycling: Saving a Glossary Entry

It's almost embarrassingly easy to save a glossary entry. First, select the text or graphic you want to save as a glossary entry. Then open the Edit menu and select the Glossary command.

You have to give your entry a name so you can find it again later. The name can contain up to 31 characters, including spaces, but I'd keep it short so it's easier to use. That's it! Click on Define.

Put It to Work

Saving Your First Glossary Entry
One of the first items you might want to save is your company's return address. First, type this address into a document:

Precision Acronyms
One ASCII Drive
14th Floor
Suite 15
Door 6
NASA Village, Florida 80056

Now select the text by dragging over it (click on the letter P in Precision, hold down the mouse button, and drag to the number 6 at the end of the ZIP code).

Once you have the address selected, open the **Edit** menu and choose the **Glossary** command. Type the name Co. Address for the glossary item. Click on the **D**efine button.

Paper or Plastic? Recycling Your Text

When you're in a document and you want to insert data from the Glossary, just follow these 100 percent recyclable steps:

Move the insertion point to the place where you want to insert the glossary item. Then open the Edit menu and choose Glossary. From the list that appears, select the glossary item to use. (You can also type the name of the glossary item instead of searching for it.)

If you remember the name of the glossary entry, you can enter a glossary item quickly. Type the name of the glossary item into your document and press **F3**.

Click on Insert or Insert As Plain Text. If you choose Insert, the glossary item retains its own formatting. If you choose Insert As Plain Text, the glossary item takes on the formatting of the surrounding text.

> ## Put It to Work
>
> **Using Your Glossary Entry**
> Move to a place in your document where you'd like to insert the company address.
>
> Open the **Edit** menu and choose the **Glossary** command. Select the glossary item Co. Address.
>
> Click on the **Insert** button, and the company address is inserted into your document.

What's Wrong with This Picture?

Bob often likes to include the phrase "call extension number" in his memos, so one day he made a glossary entry. He typed the words into his document, selected them, and then saved them under the glossary name "Ext."

The next day, Bob was writing a memo and he decided he'd insert his pet phrase. So he typed

If you have any questions concerning this matter, 231.

Then he moved the insertion point to the 2 in 231 and inserted his glossary entry. It came out as

If you have any questions concerning this matter, call extension number231.

What can Bob do so he doesn't need to type the extra space all the time?

Answer: Bob can save the space as part of the glossary entry. He should select the entry with the space included, and redefine the glossary entry (as explained in the next section).

Correcting Your Glossary Mistakes

You can modify or delete your glossary entries later on as needed.

To modify an entry, insert it into your document and make your changes. Select the new version in your document, and then open the Edit menu and choose Glossary. From the list, select the glossary item that you want to redefine. Click on the **Define** button. Word will ask you if you really want to redefine the glossary entry. Click on Yes. It's as easy as that!

Put It to Work

Making a Change to a Glossary Item
Let's say you wanted to dress up your company address to make it stand out a bit more. Select the company name, Precision Acronyms, and increase its point size by two points. (Use the Ribbon to change the point size quickly.) Then make the company name italic by clicking on the **Italic** button on the Ribbon.

Select the entire address and open the **Edit** menu. Choose the Glossary command. Select the item Co. Address and click on the **Define** button. Click on the **Yes** button, and the glossary item will be changed.

If you want to delete an entry you no longer use, it's a similar procedure. Open the Edit menu and choose Glossary (again!). Select the glossary item that you want to delete, and then click on the **Delete** button. Delete more entries if you want, or click on the **Close** button to close the dialog box.

The Least You Need to Know

Here's a quick gloss over the important items in this chapter:

- ☛ To save text or graphics in the Glossary, select the item you want to store and then open the **Edit** menu. Choose Glossary. Enter a name for the item, and click on the **Define** button.

continues

continued

☞ To use your glossary, move the insertion point to the place where you want to insert the glossary item. Open the **Edit** menu and select Glossary. Click on **Insert** to retain the item's formatting, or click on Insert As Plain **T**ext to have the item take on the formatting of surrounding text.

☞ If you want to change the glossary item later on, make your changes in the document and then open the **Edit** menu. Choose Glossary and type the name of the item to redefine. Click on **D**efine.

☞ To delete a glossary item, open the **Edit** menu and choose Glossary. Select the item to delete and click on the Delete button.

Part III
Other Stuff You Paid for but Never Knew How to Use

Yes, I am one of the millions of Americans who own one of those new handi-cams (that's a video camera that was left in the dryer too long). Anyway, it comes "full-featured," which is a nice way of saying that there are entirely too many buttons on it. I've had the camera for a year and I only know what the ON button is for.

Maybe you've been using Word like I use my handi-cam: just point and shoot—never mind the fine-tuning. There's nothing wrong with that; I've got a shelf full of videos to prove it. But when you're ready to know what "all those other buttons are for," come back and read this section.

Chapter 18
Templates: Creating "Paint by Number" Documents

In This Chapter

☛ What is a template?

☛ How to use a template

☛ Changing your document's template

☛ Using Word's custom templates

☛ Creating your own templates

The one thing that most of us don't have in excess is time. If you want to send a business letter, you have to

☛ Open a new document.

☛ Set the page margins, paper size, and orientation.

☛ Create headers and footers (such as a company logo or a page number).

☛ Enter the addresses and the salutation.

But with *templates*, most of this groundwork would already be done for you. I guess that's why I like them: templates help fill the emptiness so I don't have to start each document from scratch. Like a paint-by-number kit that provides a rough outline, a template acts as a pattern for your document.

Template Defines the environment for a document, such as margin settings, page orientation, and so on. Word for Windows comes with additional templates that you can use to create specialized documents. If you are using one of these templates, your screen may look different from the ones shown in this book.

Boilerplate text Generic text (such as a standard greeting or a return address) that's saved as part of a template so it doesn't have to be retyped into every document that uses that template.

To Template or Not to Template

Even with that great intro, you're probably thinking: "I don't need no stinkin' templates." Okay, templates are a potentially boring topic, so I can understand your reluctance to learn more about them. But hang in there; templates, although not as interesting as the Elvis stamp controversy, can still do some pretty fantastic things.

The purpose behind templates is based on a simple idea: although you may do a lot of work in Word, you probably create *only a few* distinct types of documents: memos, business letters, reports, and proposals. So when you use a template, most of the up-front formatting work is already done, and you're ready to type the text for *the current* memo, letter, report, or proposal.

A template can be constructed for each of these types of documents with margin settings, paper size, and other information already selected. In addition, you can save some *boilerplate text* in the template, such as a return address, a greeting, and a salutation, to save time in creating documents of that type. A template can also store the styles you've defined, as well as glossary entries you've saved.

For example, a template for business correspondence might have "holes" in it for the recipient's address, the salutation ("Dear John:"), and the closing ("Most respectfully yours"). A template for personal correspondence would have similar "holes" for the address and the salutation ("Dear *whomever:*") and might even have some boilerplate text: "You are the most important person in my life, *whomever*, and I feel that while I profess my love for you, we must sit down soon and work out property distribution arrangements. . . ." (The previous sentence was suggested by my ex-boyfriend.)

But templates are more than just a stencil for a document that you "fill" with text. Your choice of templates affects which commands are available on the menus and which tools are displayed on the Toolbar.

Generic Is Not Always Better

Once, in order to save some money, my sister tried some generic pasta. Well, needless to say, my sister soon discovered that the pasta tasted about as good as the box it came in. Not that it was all that bad, it just wasn't all that great either.

Word comes with its own generic: the Normal template. Unless you switch templates when you start a new document, your document is based on the Normal template. But keep in mind that because it's generic, the Normal template doesn't come with anything special to help you get work done on a specific document. Word comes with many other templates, each designed for a specific purpose, such as reports, newsletters, and so on.

Selecting a Template for Your Document

You'll learn about each of the Word templates in just a moment. But for now, suppose you wanted to use one of the Word templates to produce a particular style of letter or for a particular type of business document. Here's what you do to select one of the Word templates when you start a new document.

First, open the File menu and select New. Under Use Template, select the template you want to use. Then click on the **OK** button. Later, when you have created your own templates, you can follow these same steps to use your templates for creating documents.

If you've already opened a document and you want to change the template it's based on, open the File menu and choose Template. Under Attach Document To, select the template you'd like to use. When you're done, click on **OK**.

Documents-by-Number: Here Come the Word Templates

Like a greeting card company, Word has a template for practically every occasion:

Letters   Word has several templates for letters, including block and modified block styles.

Memos   Word has a single memo template that follows a standard memo format.

Reports   Word has several templates for reports, including reports in portrait and landscape styles, a report with headings in the margins, and a business proposal.

Other templates   Additional templates include one for a dissertation, a fax cover sheet, a press release, a term paper, a magazine article, and mailing labels.

> ### By the Way . . .
>
> In Chapter 23, you'll find a complete description of every Word template, along with a candid snapshot of each one. So you won't have any trouble selecting your favorite template when you start a new document, the name of each template is also included in Chapter 23.

Look on the Format menu for an Instructions command; it provides details on how to best use the template to complete your document, or turn to Chapter 23 for additional help.

After you select one of these templates for a new document, you'll probably see a box asking you for information needed to complete the document, such as the name of the report.

You can create your own templates or customize the ones that come with Word for Windows. The Word templates typically have additional commands available on the menus that allow you to work with them more efficiently. Most of the templates come with specialized commands located on the Format menu, such as Update Title Information.

Creating Your Own Templates

You can create your own template based on an existing document by opening that document, and then following along with this procedure.

First, delete any text you don't want to reuse in other documents. Verify that the document settings, such as margins, columns, and page orientation, are set the way you want to save them. Create common text elements, such as headers, footers, or headings. You may also want to create the styles you'll want to use when designing a document based on this template. Once your template is ready, save it.

To save your template, open the File menu and choose the Save As command. Enter a name for the template, using a name that describes the template's purpose, such as SALESRPT. Under Save File as Type, select **Document Template**.

Put It to Work

Using a Template to Create a Document

So that you can understand the extent to which templates simplify the task of creating a document, let's walk through the process of creating a document based on one of Word's templates, LETBLOCK.

First, open the **File** menu and select **New**. In the Template box, select **LETBLOCK**. You'll see a series of dialog boxes that lead you through the process of creating a letter: entering your address, entering the recipient's address, and so on. (A PC guru can help you customize your templates to work this way, too, using a programming language called WordBasic that is part of Word.)

After the basic information has been entered, all the robotics will stop and give you a chance to type your letter. Like all of the Word templates, you'll find additional commands on the Format menu, such as Instructions, Create Mailing Label, and so on.

The Least You Need to Know

Here's a paint-by-number guide for using templates:

- ☞ To see which template you are using, choose the **T**emplate command on the **F**ile menu.

- ☞ When you create a new document, select the template to use in the **U**se Template list box.

- ☞ To change the template your document is using, open the **F**ile menu and select the **T**emplate command. Under Attach **D**ocument To, select the template you'd like to use.

- ☞ If you use one of Word's custom templates, look for special commands, such as **I**nstructions on the Forma**t** menu.

- ☞ You can create a template based on a document by opening the **F**ile menu and choosing the Save **A**s command. Enter the name for the template, then select **Document Template** under Save File as Type.

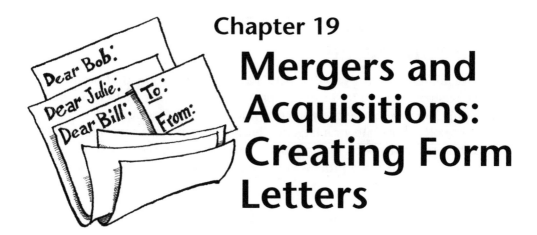

Chapter 19

Mergers and Acquisitions: Creating Form Letters

In This Chapter

- ☛ The magical world of merging
- ☛ Creating a data file
- ☛ Writing your dummy letter
- ☛ Merging to create form letters

About 6 months ago, I was reading one of the magazines I subscribe to when I spotted an ad with my name in it. The ad read, "If you've been thinking of buying a computer, Jennifer Flynn, now is the time." I must have stared at that for at least a few minutes. I mean, how did they get my name there?

Then it hit me—it was just another variation of the old form letter. You would've thought that I was over the thrill of seeing my name in a *personalized* letter. I mean, who really believes that "you may have already won!"?

But there's no denying that form letters and mailing labels are two of the best reasons for typing your letters on a computer, so let's see how this computer magic is done.

Some Basics You Should Know Before You Merge

First of all, let me warn you that this is a very boring topic that produces some real cool results: for example, print 200 personalized letters when you only type *one*. So before you continue, get a caffeine equivalent (coffee, cola, chocolate, or a large mallet), some aspirin, a ton of letterhead, and then prop this book up someplace where you can see it as you work. Believe me, this is not a process you'll want to *memorize*. All set? Okay, let's go!

Merge   Known also as *mail merge*. This is the process of taking a generic document and blending it with another document that contains variable information (such as names and addresses) in order to create *multiple documents* (such as form letters or mailing labels).

In order to create form letters or mailing labels in Word, you need two files: a *main document* file that contains the generic text and formatting (such as margin settings, paper size, and the like) that should appear in every copy of the final document, and a *data file* that contains the variable information (such as the individual names and addresses). The process of taking the names and addresses from the data file and mixing them into the main document to create multiple form letters (or mailing labels) is called *merging*.

Still awake? Well, you're almost past the worst of the boring background stuff. Just one more section to go before you get to do something.

That's One for the Record

The data file contains the stuff that changes with each form letter or each mailing label. For example, if you wanted to send a letter to each of your customers, the data file (or data document if you prefer) would contain each customer's name, address, and maybe even a customer number.

Field names

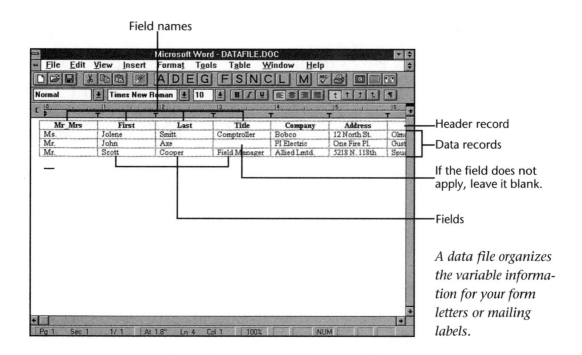

Header record

Data records

If the field does not apply, leave it blank.

Fields

A data file organizes the variable information for your form letters or mailing labels.

In your customer data file, each individual client would represent a *data record*. A data record is a collection of the related information about that specific client: his name, address, phone number, and client account number. Each client would have his own record in the data file.

The individual pieces that make up a data record are called *fields*. For example, the client's name would be one field, while the address would be another. Each field has its own name—for example, the client name field could be called NAME, and the account number field could be called ACCOUNT (clever, eh?). The names for each field are stored in the *header record*, which is usually just the first line in the data file.

Giving Birth to a Data File

Before you create your data file, think about how you are going to use the individual fields. For example, in a typical business letter, you usually include the client's full name and address:

Mr. George Blabberton
Chief Cook and Bottle Washer
Universal Foods, Incorporated
210 W. 86th Street
Piggstown, Vt. 31209

But in the greeting, you can get more friendly:

Dear George,

However, if you create a NAME field which contains the client's entire name, you'll be stuck with a greeting like this:

Dear Mr. George Blabberton,

It's just a guess, but I think that with this greeting, even Mr. George Blabberton would be able to figure out he'd just received a form letter. So instead, break the client's name into several parts: Mr_Mrs, Firstname, and Lastname.

Something else to think about: will you want to sort the data file's records in any particular order before creating your form letters or mailing labels? Even though it may make sense to have one field for a client's entire address, you can't sort by town or ZIP code unless each of these is its own field. (You can't sort on something that's *part* of a field.) In this case, you will want to create separate fields for the parts of an address: Address, City, State, and ZIP.

At Last! Creating the Data File

Well, I've given you enough to think about; let's get down to business! To create a data file, follow these steps. (If you want some hands-on practice rather than some generic steps, skip ahead to the Put It to Work exercise. When you're ready to create your own data file, come back to this section.)

 Click on the **New** button on the Toolbar to create a new document. Open the File menu and select Print **Merge**. Then click on Attach Data File and on Create Data File.

Now you're ready to add the field names for your data file. In the Field Name box, type the name for the first field (for example, Mr_Mrs). A field name can consist of 32 characters, but *no spaces* (use an underscore like I did to substitute for a space if you want to use one).

When you're ready to add another field into the data file, click on the Add button. Type the name for the second field in the Field Name box (for example, First). Click on the Add button again. Repeat this process for all the fields you want to use. It doesn't matter what order you enter the fields in; you can use them in your document in any order.

When you're done, click on **OK**, and then enter a name for your data file. If you were creating a client address data file, you could call it something clever like ADDRESS or CLIENTS, but just remember that file names are limited to eight characters. Click on **OK** again, and Word creates a table in your data file document. Now you're ready to enter the variable information into your data file.

Put It to Work

Creating a Sample Data File
Let's create a small data file as practice. Click on the **New** button on the Toolbar to open a new document (just use the NORMAL template). Open the **F**ile menu and select Print Merge. Click on Attach **D**ata File and then **C**reate Data File.

Enter these field names, clicking on the **A**dd button after each one:

Mr_Mrs
First
Last
Title
Company
Address
City
State
ZIP

After entering the field names, click on the **OK** button. Enter **TEST** as a name for your data file and click on **OK**. Congrats! Your data file is created and waiting for you to enter some data (which you'll do as soon as you learn how).

Filling in the Blanks

Entering information into the data file is the same as entering data into any other table. (Look back at Chapter 15 if you don't know how.) Here are some tips for entering data into the data file:

- ☞ It's okay if the text wraps inside one of the cells; it won't affect how that text appears in your document.

- ☞ Press **Tab** to move to the next field or **Shift+Tab** to move backwards.

- ☞ If a field does not apply for a particular record (for example, you don't know a client's title), leave it blank by pressing **Tab** to bypass it.

- ☞ If you want to type several paragraphs in the cell, press **Enter** at the end of each paragraph as you would at any other time. You don't have to limit your database to just names and addresses; it can include whole paragraphs as well.

- ☞ 📄 When you're through entering data, click on the **Save** button on the Toolbar to save the data file.

Put It to Work

Entering Our Sample Data File's Variable Information
Starting with the first field of our test data file, enter these client records. (If a field doesn't apply, press **Tab** to move to the next field. Don't try to space over with the Spacebar.)

Mr_Mrs	First	Last	Title	Company
Ms.	Jolene	Smitt	Comptroller	Bobco
Mr.	John	Axe		PI Electric
Mr.	Scott	Cooper	Field Manager	Allied Lmtd.

Address	City	State	ZIP
12 North St.	Olmo	OK	73521
One Fire Pl.	Guston	NJ	07401
5218 N. 118th	Spud	IN	83318

> Click on the **Save** button on the Toolbar to save the file. (You can enter summary information for the data file if you want.)

Creating a Dummy Letter

Now we get to have fun. First, let me tell you the steps for creating a form letter and then we'll do one together.

Click on the **New** button on the Toolbar to create a new document for the dummy letter. Next, attach your data file to the dummy letter file. Then open the **File** menu and select Print Merge. Click on Attach **Data File**, select your data file, and then click on **OK**. Start entering the text for the document.

When you get to the place where you need to insert a field from the data file, click on the Insert Merge Field button on the Print Merge bar. In the **Print Merge Fields** list box, choose the field you want to insert and click on **OK**. In your document, you'll see something like <<First>>, which represents the inserted field.

Keep entering text and inserting field codes until the letter is done. When you're done with your form letter, save it by clicking on the **Save** button on the Toolbar.

> ## By the Way . . .
> Remember to add spaces between field codes when necessary. When I was setting up the sample that you're about to do, I got in a hurry and forgot to insert a space between the field codes for the first and last names. So check your form letter carefully before you perform the actual merge and have hundreds of them to correct.

Put It to Work

Creating Our Form Letter

Let's create a simple form letter for practice:

 Click on the **New** button on the Toolbar. Attach the data file by opening the **File** menu and selecting Print Merge. Click on Attach **D**ata File, select your data file, and click on **OK**.

Start by inserting the client address fields: click on the Insert Merge **F**ield button and insert the Mr_Mrs field. Press the **Spacebar**, insert the First field, press the **Spacebar** again, and insert the Last field. Press **Enter**.

Insert the Title field and press **Enter**. Insert the rest of the address fields, each on its own line (except for the City, State, and ZIP fields).

Now press **Enter** four times to insert some space between the address and the greeting. Type **Dearest**, press the **Spacebar**, and insert the First field. Add a comma and then press **Enter** twice.

Type the body of your letter:

You may have already won 1 million dollars! To obtain a complete list of winners, send $100 in small unmarked bills to me. Thank you and come again.

 Click on the **Save** button on the Toolbar and save your form letter. Call it PHONEY or something equally as clever.

The Fat Lady Sings: Merging the Data File with the Dummy Letter

Finally! Congratulations on making it to our final act: merging the data file with the dummy letter to create form letters. This part is really easy, as you'll soon see.

You have two choices at this point. All you've got to do is to click the appropriate button on the Print Merge bar.

☛  You can merge the files and create one big file that you can print later (each form letter will appear in the file on its own page).

☛ You can merge the files together and print the form letters now.

Put It to Work

Merging Our Sample Files
If you want, turn on your printer. Then click on the **Print Merge File** button on the Print Merge bar and print your form letters. It's as simple as that!

You can create mailing labels with your data file, but the process is a bit involved, so you may want to ask a PC guru for help. If this little warning hasn't deterred you and you want to try it yourself, read Chapter 22.

The Least You Need to Know

Congratulations! You have won several million dollars worth of wonderful tips on merging files:

☛ A *record* is a collection of related information about a single person or thing, such as a client. The individual pieces that make up a record are called *fields*.

☛ To create a data file, click on the **New** button to create a new document. Open the **File** menu and select Print **Merge**. Click on Attach

continues

continued

Data File and then **C**reate Data File. Add the names for each field in the **F**ield Name box, clicking on the **A**dd button to add each field. When you're done, click on **OK** and enter a name for the data file. Click on **OK** again.

☛ Enter data into the table by pressing **Tab** to move from field to field.

☛ To create a form letter, start by clicking on the **New** button on the Toolbar. Attach the data file by opening the **F**ile menu and selecting Print **M**erge. Click on Attach **D**ata File, select your data file, and click on **OK**. Type the text of the letter. When you need to insert a field into the letter, click on the Insert Merge **F**ield button and select the field name from the **P**rint Merge Fields list box.

☛ To merge the data file with the form letter, click on either the **Print Merge File** or the **Create Merge File** button on the Print Merge bar.

Chapter 20

Extra! Extra! Read All About Columns!

In This Chapter

- ☞ The difference between a table and a column
- ☞ How to add newspaper-style columns to a document
- ☞ Deciding which view mode to use when working with columns
- ☞ Adding vertical lines between columns

I'll let you in on a little secret: *columns* are not just for newsletters anymore. This may shock those of you who thought you would just skip this chapter because you don't write the company newsletter, but columns are found in some of the better documents the world over. For example, you might use columns to add interest to a report by splitting the document into two columns—a skinny one on the left for short summaries of major points and a fatter one on the right for your actual report. And what better way to format an index than to use two columns?

Newspaper-style columns Similar to the style of column found in newspapers. Text in these columns flows between invisible boundaries down one part of the page. At the end of the page, the text continues at the top of the next column.

A different type of column is the *parallel column,* which is just a fancy way of saying "table." With a table, you read *across* (instead of down) several columns of text and numbers. If you want to "set a table" into your document instead of creating newspaper-style columns, see Chapter 15.

Section   A part of a document that has different settings from the main document for things such as the number of columns, as well as margins, paper size, headers, footers, and page numbering. A section can be of any length: from several pages to several para-graphs—or even a single line (such as a masthead for your newsletter).

This Just In: What You Should Know About Using Columns

Newspaper-style columns are like those you find in your hometown newspaper. Columns can be "interrupted" by graphics (pictures or charts) that illustrate the story being told. (You'll learn how to insert graphics and other objects into a document in Chapter 21.)

When you start a new document, you are typing text into a *single column* that stretches the width of the margins. At any point in your document, you can change the number of columns by creating a *section.*

When you add columns to a document, the width of the columns is automatically adjusted so they fit equally between the margins. For instance, if you add three columns, the width of your paper is divided into three equal parts.

By the Way . . .

If you want your document to contain columns of varying widths, I have bad news: there is no easy way to do this in Word for Windows, and personally, I wouldn't even try. (Instead, I'd use a desktop publishing program, such as PageMaker or Ventura Publisher.)

Reading the Fine Print: Viewing Column Layout

Each viewing mode displays columns a little differently, with each mode offering its own advantages. For example, in Normal view, you can enter text faster than in other views, but your document will look like it's on drugs. Although you may have four columns set up, in Normal view, the text will be displayed in one long column running along the left side of the page. To switch to Normal view, open the **View** menu and choose the **Normal** command.

Switch to Page Layout view to see how your columns will really look when printed. Use this view to make final adjustments to text and column widths. To switch to Page Layout view, open the **View** menu and choose the **Page Layout** command.

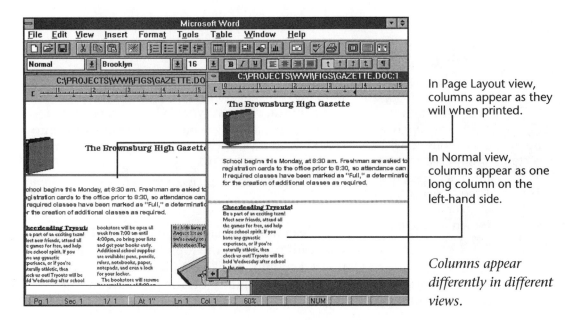

In Page Layout view, columns appear as they will when printed.

In Normal view, columns appear as one long column on the left-hand side.

Columns appear differently in different views.

Within either Normal or Page Layout view, you can zoom in (to get a closer look at text) or zoom out (to get an overview of the page layout). Use one of these buttons on the Toolbar:

 Zoom Whole Page   This displays an entire page of your document on-screen.

 Zoom 100 Percent   This displays your document in its normal size.

 Zoom Page Width   This "Up Close and Personal" view displays both margins of your document on-screen. When you use this mode, the text fills the screen from side to side.

Gossip Column: How to Insert Columns into Your Document

Here's Miss Mayflower (our gossip columnist) with the latest on inserting columns into your document. (Stay tuned for an update on a recent Elvis spotting.) First, move to the *section* in the document where you'd like to change the number of columns. If you need to create a section break so you don't affect earlier text, open the Forma**t** menu and select Columns. Type the number of columns you want and select **This Point Forward** in the Apply To list box. Click on **OK**.

If you just want to change the current number of columns in this section, simply click on the **Text Column** button on the Toolbar. Drag to select the number of columns you want, and then release the mouse button.

Miss Mayflower Discusses How to Enter Text

Miss Mayflower says that if you want to enter text in a column, you just type. When you reach the bottom of a page, text will automatically flow into the next column. If you want to force a paragraph to start at the top of the next column before you reach the bottom of a page, you can insert a *column break*.

For example, perhaps you have a heading that you want to start at the top of the next column. To insert a column break, just place the insertion point where you want to start a new column (on the first letter of the column heading, for example) and press **Ctrl+Shift+Enter**.

What's Wrong with This Picture?

Irene wanted her two-page report to have two columns on the first page and three columns on the second. After creating two columns and typing the text for page one, Irene changed to three-column format on page two. When she had completed her report, she went back to look at page one and saw to her horror that it had mysteriously changed to three columns. What should she do?

Answer: Irene must have used the Text Columns button on the Toolbar to switch from two- to three-column format. The Text Columns button changes the number of columns for the current section, but does not create a section break. Irene should have used the Columns command on the Format menu instead, because it can create section breaks. What Irene should do now is use the Insert Break command to insert a section break.

Pinstriping Your Columns

You can add a vertical line (I think of it as a pinstripe) between columns, but when you do, don't be surprised if it doesn't show up. The vertical lines will appear only on the Print Preview screen. So go there to see how your columns will look.

Okay, here's what you do to pinstripe your columns. First, move to the section where you want to add lines. Open the Format menu and select Columns. Then click in the Line Between check box. Using the Apply To box, select how much of the document you want to affect.

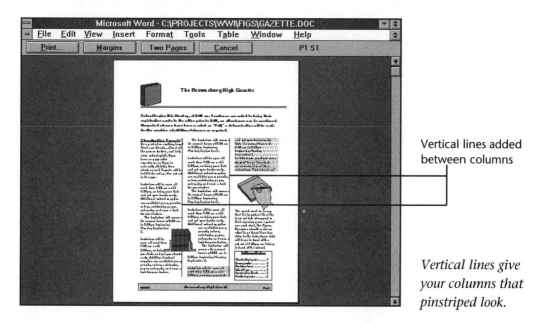

Vertical lines added between columns

Vertical lines give your columns that pinstriped look.

By the Way . . .

The vertical lines option will place lines between all the columns in that section. There is no way, for example, to place a line between two columns in a three-column section using this option. This and the fact that you can't create columns of unequal widths are just two of the reasons why you probably won't be happy using Word for Windows to create a newsletter or any document with anything other than simple columns. But if you insist, you can add interest (as I did) to a newsletter by placing borders or shading (or both) around paragraphs. I'll be glad to show you how to do that as soon as I get done with this rather bogus chapter on columns and what they don't do in Word for Windows. Actually, I think you'll like borders and shading (if you can hang on until the next chapter). They're pretty cool and a lot more fun than creating columns in Word for Windows.

The Great Balancing Act

At the end of your document, you might want to balance (make even) the text in your columns. For example, if you're using two columns, and on the last page of your document the left column is full and the right one contains one paragraph, you might want to redistribute the text between the two columns so that they end at the same point on the page (they look even or balanced).

This is easy to do—simply insert a section break at the end of the document. First, open the **Insert** menu and select **Break**. Under Section Break, choose **Continuous**, and then click on **OK**.

The Least You Need to Know

Probably the very least you need to know is that Word for Windows is not a desktop publishing program. What you can do with Word and columns is pretty limited, but with a lot of patience, you can turn out a fairly respectable newsletter. Just remember these things:

- ☞ In newspaper-style columns, text flows from one column to the next when it reaches the bottom of a page. In a table, text is read across.

- ☞ To vary the number of columns within a document, create a new section by opening the Format menu and selecting Columns. Type the number of columns you'd like and select **This Point Forward** in the Apply To list box. Click on **OK** when you're through.

- ☞ Columns within a section are of equal width. There is no way to vary the width of columns within the same section.

- ☞ Use Normal mode to enter text into a column—it's faster. Use Page Layout mode to see how your columns will look when printed.

- ☞ To force text to start at the top of the next column, insert a column break by pressing **Ctrl+Shift+Enter**.

- ☞ You can add vertical lines between all the columns in a section by opening the Format menu and selecting Columns. Click in the Line Between check box, and select how much of the document you want to use with the Apply To list box.

This page unintentionally left blank.

Chapter 21
1001 Great Document Decorating Ideas

In This Chapter

- ☞ Adding borders and shading
- ☞ Importing graphics, text, charts, tables, and other objects
- ☞ Resizing a graphic
- ☞ Placing a frame around text or a graphic
- ☞ Moving or resizing a frame
- ☞ Controlling how text flows around a frame

My mother always told me "a house is not a home until you make it yours." The same is true about documents; I just love adding a chart here or a picture there to "dress things up."

Of course, you should avoid "over-decorating" your document. If you dress your document up with too much shading or too many borders and frames, your reader won't be able to spot your point through all that glitter.

On the other hand, you shouldn't choose just one technique (such as shading) and use it everywhere in your document. I once baby-sat for a lady who loved owls and had them all over her house: little owls, big owls, owl wallpaper, owl salt and pepper shakers, and even owl toilet paper.

(I'll never know where she found that!) I couldn't help but think I was being watched—but whooo? Whoooo?

To avoid the owlish look in your documents, you might want to vary your decorating with several techniques (shading, borders, text frames, and graphics) to avoid overloading your reader with one type of formatting.

Your Text Is Surrounded!

Borders and shading are two of my favorite ways to emphasize important text. *Borders* are lines placed on any (or all) of the four sides of a text paragraph, the cells in a table, or a graphic (a picture or a chart). *Shading* is a box of gray (or color, if you use a color printer) that forms a background for the text or cells in a table. (You can't use shading as a background for a graphic.)

Use a box border to frame text or charts.

You can do a lot with a little when you use borders and shading to emphasize the important parts of your documents.

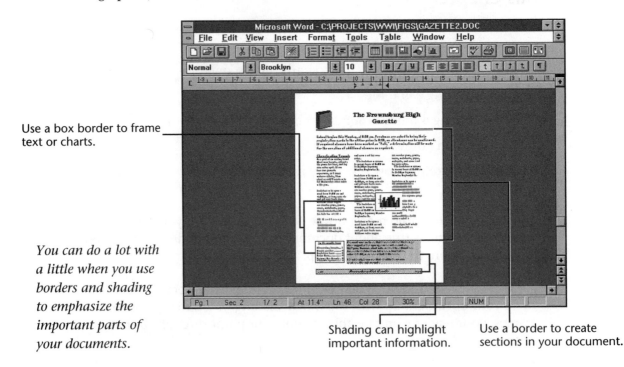

Shading can highlight important information.

Use a border to create sections in your document.

Across the Border

Placing a border around text or a graphic is fairly easy: first, select the text or graphic item to which you want to apply a border. You can select text or cells by dragging over them, or a graphic (a picture or a chart) by clicking on it.

After making your selection, open the Format menu and select **B**order. On the right-hand side of the dialog box, you'll see a make-believe page with two paragraphs. The selections you make will be represented here as a sample. If you want a box (a border around all four sides), a shadow, or a grid (if you're adding a border to a table), click on that option under Preset, and then select the type of **L**ine you'd like to use. For example, under Preset, click on **Box** and then select a thick line, and you'll see a thick box border placed around the sample paragraphs. If you like what you see, click on **OK**. If not, try another line type.

> To save time, you can add borders or shading to particular styles within your documents, instead of formatting each paragraph. To do so, open the Format menu and select the Style command. Under **S**tyle Name, select the style you want to add borders or shading to. Click on the **D**efine button and then click on **B**order. At this point, you can follow the steps in either of these two sections to add borders or shading to the style.

If placing a border around all four sides of your text makes you feel "boxed in," you can add a border on only one, two, or three sides. But to do this, you've got to make your selections in a different order. First, click on the appropriate sides to select them in the Border area. For example, to add a border that runs underneath the selected text, click on the bottom border line on the sample. You'll notice that when you do this, both ends of that border line are marked with arrows. The arrows indicate which borders you want to affect. You can even click between the paragraphs to add a border between them. Once you've selected which sides of the paragraphs you want to add a border to, select the type of **L**ine you'd like to use. When you're through making your selections, click on **OK**.

By the Way . . .

If you want to remove a border later on, select the same text or graphic, open the Format menu, and select **B**order. Click on **N**one and then click on the **OK** button.

Sporting Some Cool Shades

You can add shading behind any text or within any cell in a table. If the paragraph you select is indented, the shading will begin at the indents. For cells in a table, the shading simply fills the cell. Here's what you do.

Select the text or the cells you want to apply shading to. Then open the Format menu and select **Border** (there's that dialog box again). Click on the **Shading** button.

Use the **Pattern** box to select the percentage of gray that you want. If your letters are small, choose a lighter percentage, say 10%. If your letters are larger, choose a higher percentage. I usually start with 20%. The result is really determined by the type of printer you have and how well it handles shading, so experiment until you get the results you want. Use a font with clean, crisp lettering, such as Arial, or apply bold formatting for better results.

By the Way . . .

If you have a color printer, you can mix the **Foreground** and **Background** colors to create interesting shades.

Okay, that's it. Click on the **OK** button to return to the Border Paragraph box, and then click on **OK** again.

You Oughta Be in Pictures!

They say that nothing says it better than a picture (except maybe some *words*). Anyway, if you want to dress up your document with a graphic (nerd word for picture) or a chart, you've got several options:

- ☛ You can create your own picture in Microsoft Draw, a drawing program that comes with Word for Windows.

- You can create a picture in some other program, such as PC Paintbrush, DrawPerfect, or CorelDRAW!.

- You can take it easy and simply buy and import some artwork (called *clip art*) drawn by someone else. Word for Windows comes with a limited selection of clip-art, but there are thousands of other clip art disks you can buy from various sources. Ask your computer dealer to help you find a nice selection.

- You can create a chart using Microsoft Graph (another program that comes with Word for Windows) or import one from your *spreadsheet* program.

Spreadsheet A computer program that organizes information in columns and rows and performs calculations. If you want to balance a checkbook or last year's budget, use a spreadsheet program. Common spreadsheets include Lotus 1-2-3, Microsoft Excel, and Quattro Pro.

Welcome to the Import Business

When you bring a graphic into your document, you *import* it. (Bet you didn't know you'd be getting into the import business.) When you import a graphic, it pretty much stays where it was placed within the document. You can move it around a little by cutting and pasting as you would text, but if you want complete control over where the graphic appears on the page, import the graphic into a *frame*. For example, if you want to place your graphic in a margin, or between columns, you're going to need a frame.

Frame A small box in which you place text or graphics so you can easily maneuver them within your document.

Importing Without Frames

You'll learn more about frames in a minute, but first let's learn the easy import method—importing without a frame.

First, move the insertion point to the spot where you'd like to place the graphic. Then open the Insert menu and select Picture. As you may have guessed, a dialog box appears.

From this dialog box, select a graphic to import. Click on the graphic file you want in the File Name box. If you'd like to see what you're getting, click on the Preview button. If you want to link your picture to the program that you used to create it, use the Link to File check box. (More on this in a moment.) When you're ready, click on **OK**.

Just a Trim, Please

If your graphic is the size of a small elephant, you can adjust its size (this is called *scaling* a graphic) or cut parts away or trim (this is called *cropping*).

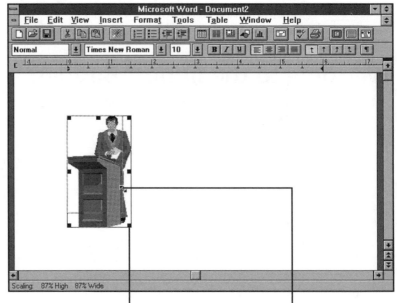

When you want to scale or crop a graphic, you grab it by one of its handles.

Grab the graphic by this handle and drag.   You'll see a box as you drag.

To scale a graphic, select it by clicking on it, and then drag one of the corner handles until the graphic is the size you want. (As you drag, you'll see a ghostly outline—but don't let that spook you!) If you drag the graphic by a side handle, you'll get a kind of "squashed" look, which may not be what you want, so it's best to use one of the corner handles.

To crop (trim) a graphic, select it by clicking on it. Press and hold the **Shift** key as you drag a handle to shrink the frame around the area of the graphic you want to keep.

If you mess up and you want to restore the graphic to its original size and shape, open the Format menu and select the Picture command. Click on Reset and then **OK** to restore the graphic.

The Ins and Outs of Linking and Embedding

When you import a graphic, you can link it to the original application you used to create it. That way, if you were to go back to that application and change the original graphic in some way, you could update the imported graphic and avoid having to import it again.

If you chose the *linking* option when you imported the graphic, and you've made some changes to your original document that you want to update in your imported graphic, open the Edit menu and select Links. Select the name of the graphic file and then click on Update Now. The graphic in your document is updated to reflect the changes you made to it.

Linking an object
Creating a connection between an imported object (such as a graphic) and its original application so that if changes are made to that object in the original application, those changes can be updated in your document.

Okay, So What's Embedding?

You have an alternative to linking a graphic (or other object)—and that's *embedding*. The difference between linking and embedding is where the actual object is stored. When you import a graphic and link it to its original application, the graphic is *not* stored as part of the document. Instead a link (or connection, if you prefer) is maintained between your document

Embedding an object Creating a connection between an object and the application in which it was created so that if changes need to be made to the object, you can access the original application (by double-clicking on the object).

and the program that created the graphic. Because the graphic is not actually part of your document, when you open that other program and make changes to the graphic, those changes are not reflected within your document until you update it. The link helps your document find the changed graphic and update the linked version of it.

With embedding, a graphic *is* stored as part of the document. However, just like in linking, there is a special connection between the document and the program that created the graphic. But this time it takes a different form. When you want to make changes to an embedded graphic, you don't go to the program that created it, but to your document. Double-click on the graphic, and you'll be escorted to the original program, where you'll work within its program window to make your changes. Finish making your changes and exit the graphics program, and you're wisked back to your document, where the graphic already reflects your changes. Unlike a linked object, an embedded object is updated immediately as soon as any changes are made. That's because you're not making changes to an object that's stored somewhere else, but to the one that's stored within the document.

To embed a graphic into your document, start with the graphics program. Select the graphic, open the Edit menu, and choose Copy. Switch to Word for Windows, open its Edit menu, and choose Paste Special. In the box that opens, make sure that the **Data Type** has been correctly identified (it will probably say either Picture or Bitmap), and then click on **Paste**. Your graphic is embedded into the document. Remember that when you want to make changes to it, just double-click on the graphic.

Get Ready for the Great Frame-Up

Normally, you can't just plunk down a graphic in the middle of a column of text and expect the text to avoid the graphic like some party crasher. If you want to place a graphic in the middle of a column or two (or three) of text, and you want your text to wrap around it neatly rather than leave gaping holes to the left or right of it, you should create a *frame* first. Text wraps easily around a frame. You can then place the graphic within the frame, which will shield the graphic from the text, and the text will never know it's there.

You also use a frame to better control where a graphic is placed in your document. For example, if you want to place your graphic in a margin or alongside a particular paragraph, you use a frame. If your document is going to be professionally printed, you can use frames as "placeholders" for pictures and other artwork that will be inserted at the print shop. You can use frames to position other objects, such as tables, charts, or even text (for example, a quote or a summary of an important point).

> **By the Way . . .**
> When you work with frames, you should use Page Layout view, because you'll be able to see exactly where a graphic is located within your document.

Which Came First, the Graphic or the Frame?

You can insert a graphic (or other object, such as a table, chart, or text) into your document and then place a frame around it, or you can insert an empty frame into your document and import a graphic (or other object) into it. Which is better? Here are some tips:

- ☞ If the graphic, table, or text is already in your document, don't sweat it now. Just place a frame around it if you want to position the object in the margins or between columns.

- ☞ If you want to retain the original size of the graphic, table, or chart, import it first and then frame it.

- ☞ If you want to make sure that the imported graphic, table, or chart is a particular size, create a frame in the size you need and then import the object.

Getting the Frame Straight

Well, you've hung in this far so I guess you're ready for the nitty-gritty on inserting frames into a document.

First, switch to Page Layout mode. (Open the **View** menu and select **Page Layout**.) Then, either select an item you want to frame, or move the insertion point to the spot where you'd like to place a frame. (To select a graphic, simply click on it.)

Next, click on the **Frame** button on the Toolbar. If you're framing a selected item, the frame will appear in your document. If you're creating an empty frame, you've got one more step. When you click on the Frame button, the mouse pointer changes to tiny cross-hairs. Move the cross hair pointer to the place where you want to locate the upper left corner of the frame-to-be. Click and drag towards the imaginary lower right corner of the frame-to-be. When you've got the size you want, release the mouse button, and you've got yourself a brand-new baby frame!

If you want to import a graphic into the frame, make sure that the frame is still selected and then open the Insert menu and select Picture. Choose the graphic file you want to import and click on **OK**. The graphic is resized to fit the frame.

By the Way . . .

When you create a frame, it has a thin border around it that you can change or remove by using the Forma**t B**order command. (Turn back a few pages if you need help with borders.) Also, if you are going to place text in the frame, don't worry. All the rules for formatting, alignment, and indentation are the same as before; just treat the text like any other text in your document. The difference is that because the text has a frame around it, you can move that text anyplace you want.

Frame Maintenance

Okay, you've got a frame, but what can you do with it? Well, to *resize* a frame, select it by clicking on it, and drag a corner handle until the frame is the size you want.

To *move* a frame, click on it to select it. Move the mouse pointer over the frame until you see it change into an arrow pointing North, South,

East, and West. Drag the frame to its new location and then let go of the mouse button. When you move a frame, whatever's in it moves too.

If you want to place your frame in an exact spot relative to some point of reference, open the Format menu and select Frame. You can align your frame horizontally (somewhere between the left and right edges of the paper) or vertically (somewhere between the top and bottom edges of the paper).

Under Horizontal, there are three reference points you can choose from: Margin, Page, or Column. For example, to position the frame so that it is centered between the left and right margins, move to the Horizontal area and select **Margin** under Relative To. Once you've chosen a reference, choose a Position relative to that reference. For example, once you've chosen Margin as your reference point, you can position the frame so that it is centered, left, right, inside, or outside of the margins.

Under Vertical, there are two reference points: Margin and Page. Follow the same steps as you would under Horizontal: select a reference (Margin or Page) and a position relative to that reference (top, center, bottom). For example, if you selected Margin and Bottom, the frame would be placed at the bottom of the page, just inside the bottom margin.

Actually, there is a third reference point under Vertical, and that's Paragraph. When you select Paragraph, your frame will move with the paragraph immediately following it in Normal view. If you enter a number under Position, the frame will *move the specified distance down* from the paragraph it is anchored to.

Keep That Text A-Flowin'

When you first insert a frame, it's set up so that the text in your document will flow (*wrap*) around the edges of the frame. You can change this if you want to be sure that text does not appear next to the frame (only above or below it).

First, make sure that you are in Page Layout view. Select the frame by clicking in it and open the Format menu. Choose the Frame command. In the Text Wrapping area, click on None and then **OK**.

If you want text to flow around a frame, and you want to adjust the space between the text and the frame, follow these same instructions and then under Horizontal or Vertical, enter a measurement in the Distance from Text box.

What's Wrong with This Picture?

Mike imported a picture of a wine glass into a document, and to make it show up better, he decided to add a border around it and add some shading. Mike used the Forma**t** Border command to make his selections. When he got back to his document, the border was there, but the background behind the wine glass was still white. What happened to his shading?

Answer: Mike forgot that you can't add shading behind a graphic. You only can place shading behind text, or within the cells of a table.

How Do I Import Text?

If you want to open an existing document that was created in another program (such as WordPerfect), click on the **Open** button on the Toolbar and select your file. Select a file type from the List Files of **Type** drop-down list box by clicking on the down arrow and then picking a type. If your file type is not listed, select **All Files** and then click on **OK**. Word will offer a guess as to which file converter it should use to open the file. Change to another file format if necessary, or click on **OK**.

You cannot copy part of a document created in a non-Windows program. You must open the entire file and let Word convert it.

If you want to copy just part of a document that was created in another Windows program, open that document and select your text. Open the Edit menu and select Copy. Switch to Word for Windows, open its Edit menu, and select **Paste**. The text may lose some formatting.

How Do I Import a Chart or Other Object?

Some charts, such as those created by Microsoft Graph and Microsoft Excel, can be imported through the Edit menu. Just switch to the other program, select the chart or other object you want to import, open the Edit menu, and select Copy.

Now switch back to Word, move the insertion point to the place where you want the chart, and open the Edit menu. If you want to link your chart to the application you used to create it, select Paste Special and click on the Paste Link button in the box that appears. If you want to embed the chart, click on the Paste button instead.

By the Way . . .

You can create and embed certain objects (such as a Microsoft Excel chart) without leaving Word for Windows. Open the **I**nsert menu and select the **O**bject command. If your program is listed, click on it and you'll be escorted to that program so you can create your "object." Exit that program, and the object will be automatically embedded into your document. As usual, you can double-click on an embedded object to make changes to it. If your program is not among those listed, you'll have to use the **E**dit **C**opy and **E**dit Paste **S**pecial commands as explained in the preceding paragraphs.

The Least You Need to Know

You're traveling into another frame of mind, a graphic dimension of linking and embedding. At the signpost up ahead, your next stop . . . the Document Zone! Submitted for your approval are these tips on graphics, borders, and shading:

continues

continued

☞ To place a border around text or a graphic, select it and then open the Format menu and choose Border. Select a border option and click on **OK**.

☞ To add shading to text or cells in a table, select what you want and then open the Format menu and choose Border. Click on Shading. Select the percentage of gray using the **P**attern box, and select a foreground and background color if you want. Click on **OK** when you're through.

☞ To import a graphic, move the insertion point to the spot where you would like to place the graphic. Open the Insert menu and select Picture. Select a graphic to import, and create a link to the original application if you want by clicking on **L**ink to File and then **OK**.

☞ To scale a graphic, select it and drag one of the corner handles. To crop a graphic, press the **Shift** key as you drag to shrink the area around the part of the graphic you want to keep.

☞ To insert a frame around text or a graphic, select it and then click on the **Frame** button on the Toolbar. To create an empty frame, click on the **Frame** button and then click in the document to establish the upper left corner of the frame. Drag to the lower right corner and release the mouse button.

☞ To prevent text from flowing around the edges of a frame, select the frame and open the Format menu. Choose Frame, and under Text Wrapping click on **N**one.

Part IV
Why I Always Stick Around for the Credits

You've seen them: those people who are still in their seats after the movie is over and the credits are rolling. You'll be halfway home while they're still waiting for the movie to end. Well, I'm one of those people—because when I watch the credits, I find out all sorts of interesting things I wouldn't have otherwise: like who the "best boy" is and where the movie was made. This section is like movie credits; it's full of all those interesting things I wanted to tell you about Word, but ran out of room for earlier.

Chapter 22

What I Was Going to Tell You, When I Ran Out of Room

In This Chapter

- ☛ Turning text upside down and every which way with cool special effects
- ☛ Adding a caption to a figure, table, or chart
- ☛ Creating a graph for a document
- ☛ Adding a drop capital to a paragraph
- ☛ Letting others add comments to your work
- ☛ Creating your own hidden reminders
- ☛ Customizing a distribution list
- ☛ Entering special characters
- ☛ Printing mailing labels

This chapter is a hodgepodge of some neat things that Word can do. Use this as a springboard for ideas—or a really good excuse to avoid opening the Word manual.

Cool Things You Can Do with Text

Word for Windows contains a program called MS WordArt allows you to do neat things with text such as

Turn it upside down.

Run it around in circles.

Put a shadow behind the text. (Scary!)

Bend the text.

Slant it up, down, more up, and more down.

Colorize text (Ted Turner, watch out!)

Put white text on a black background.

So how do you create all this loveliness? Well, first, move to the place in your document where you'd like to add some special text. Open the Insert menu and select Object, and one of those dialog boxes will open. If you want, change the font and point size, then type your text.

Under Style, choose from upside down, button (circle), slant up, slant more, slant down, or slant less. Under Align, you can center, left-, or right-align text. You can also add spaces between letters or words to justify the text.

If you want color text or white text on a black background, use Fill. The color you choose with Fill is the color of the text. If you want a color background, use the Color Background check box. Add shadow effects with the Shadow check box.

When you're done, click on **OK**. If you want to move the text to a particular spot within your document, add a frame by clicking on the **Frame** button. Then drag the text wherever you want.

Adding a Caption to a Figure, Table, or a Chart

Adding a caption to a figure (a graphic) allows you to make a simple statement that summarizes your point.

If your caption is long, don't worry; the text wraps within the margins of the object automatically.

By the Way . . .

I've been adding captions throughout this book whenever I include a picture. Captions help summarize your point, so the reader knows what to look at in the figure, table, or chart.

Adding a caption to a figure, table, or chart is relatively easy. Start by clicking on the object to select it. Press **Enter** and you're ready to type your caption.

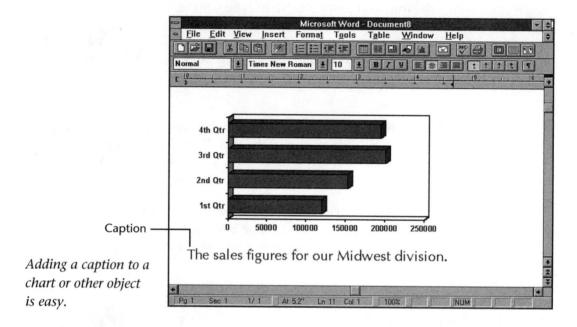

Adding a caption to a chart or other object is easy.

Graphing Your Ideas

Word for Windows includes a simple tool to create graphs called (cleverly enough) Microsoft Graph. If you already use Lotus 1-2-3 or Microsoft Excel, you can import your data from those *spreadsheets* instead of using WordGraph. See Chapter 21 for help.

To create a graph, first move to the place in the document where you want to insert a graph. Then start Microsoft Graph by clicking on the **Graph** button. You'll see some fake data already entered; this makes it easier to figure out how to enter your own data.

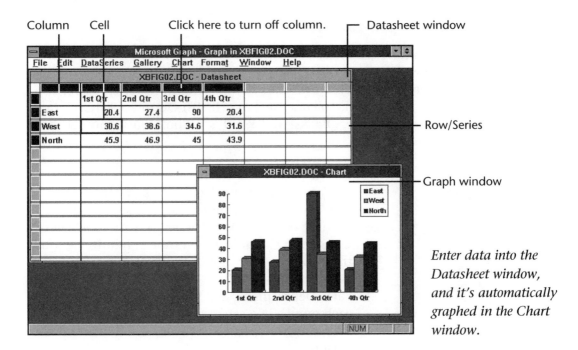

Column   Cell   Click here to turn off column.   Datasheet window

Row/Series

Graph window

Enter data into the Datasheet window, and it's automatically graphed in the Chart window.

Row titles   These titles represent each *series*. A series is a collection of related data—for example, the travel expenses for one year for a single salesperson. Additional salespeople are represented by additional rows; each row is considered a series.

Column titles   These titles represent a single point in time, such as January or February or 1992 or 1993.

Cell   Here's where the values go.

There are a lot more terms I could throw at you, but the only thing that will make any sense is simply creating your first graph. So let's get to it. Suppose you wanted to graph the travel expenses for your sales department for each month of the first quarter.

Spreadsheet   A computer program that organizes information in columns and rows and performs calculations. If you want to balance a checkbook or last year's budget, use a spreadsheet program. Common spreadsheets include Lotus 1-2-3, Microsoft Excel, and Quattro Pro.

Oh, Boy, a Sample Chart!

The points in time are entered across the top of the datasheet as column titles. Begin with the cell that says 1st Qtr, and type **January**, **February**, **March**. To enter them, type over the existing column headings, using **Tab** to move from cell to cell. To erase the last cell, 4th Qtr, press **Tab** to move to that cell and then press **Backspace**. You'll see a box—just ignore it and press **Enter**.

To turn off a row or a column so that it does not affect the graph, double-click on the button at the front of that row or column.

The names of the series are entered along the left-hand side of the datasheet as row titles. You don't have to have more than one series. (After all, we have only *one* World Series, so why spoil a good thing?) For example, if you were graphing the total travel expenses by month for the entire sales department, you'd have only one series (row) called **Sales Department**, and you'd enter the data for each month in a separate column. If you want to break the total expenses down by salesperson as we do, you'll need a row (or series) for each salesperson.

What You Want Is What You Get

Microsoft Graph automatically graphs your data as a column chart, but you can use other chart types instead. Here's what each chart type might be best suited for:

If you don't want a legend in your chart (that little box that explains what each series stands for), simply click on it and press **Delete**. If you don't like where the legend was placed, click on it to select it and then drag it wherever you'd like.

Column   Compares values at a given point in time.

Bar   Like a sideways column chart; use this just like a column chart to compare values at a given point in time.

Line   Emphasizes trends and changing values over time.

Area   Like a filled-in line chart; use this just like a line chart to emphasize changing values.

Pie   Use this to show the relationship between parts of a whole.

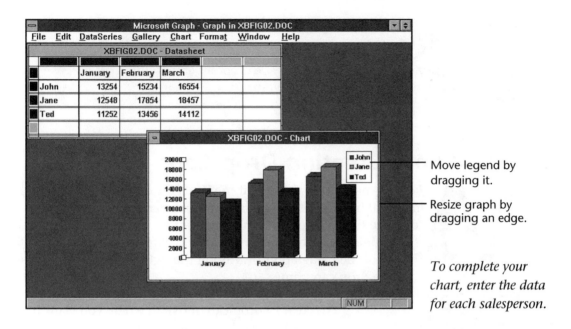

Move legend by dragging it.

Resize graph by dragging an edge.

To complete your chart, enter the data for each salesperson.

I used a 3-D column for my sample chart, but you may prefer something else. To change the chart type, open the **Gallery** menu and choose the chart type you want. You'll see varieties of the chart type you chose; just select one of the available varieties and click on **OK**.

> ## By the Way . . .
>
> After your graph is complete, you can resize it by dragging the edge of the graph window. You can also resize a graph after it is inserted into your Word document.

Copying Your Great-Looking Chart into a Word Document

Well, you're almost done. Now all you have to do is copy the completed chart into your document. Open the File menu and select Exit and Return to Document. Your chart will be embedded at the point in your document where you activated Microsoft Graph. Because it's an *embedded object*, just double-click on the graph to edit it.

> ## By the Way . . .
>
> In your document, you can add a border around the chart by using the **Format Border** command.

Instant Epic: Creating Drop Caps

A drop cap, now that I think of it, reminds me of those ornate medieval bibles where the first letter of a verse was always two or three times larger than the other letters. The top of a drop cap lines up with the first line of the paragraph, and the text of the paragraph flows along the right side and bottom of the drop-cap frame.

Embedded object   An object (such as a chart or a graphic) that maintains a link to the program that created it. Embedded objects are stored with your document, unlike linked objects, which are stored separately. If you want to change an embedded object, just double-click on it.

To create a drop cap, move to where you want to place it, open the Insert menu, and select Object. Select **MS WordArt**, and a dialog box will pop up.

From here, change the font and point size if you want, and then type the first letter of the paragraph. Under Align, choose **Center**. Then choose **OK**. You'll see the drop cap in your document. It may be way too large; don't worry, we'll take care of that later.

If you haven't typed your paragraph, go ahead and do it. When you're through, switch to Page Layout view.

To size the letter, we're going to need it to be framed. (Chapter 21 covered frames and sizing.) Select the drop cap by clicking on it and then place a frame around it by clicking on the **Frame** button.

Drop cap   A *drop cap* (or dropped capital as Word calls it) is used to set off the first letter in a paragraph. The letter is enlarged and set into the text of the paragraph, at its upper left-hand corner.

Resize the drop cap as necessary by dragging a corner handle. Once the drop cap is the size you want, move the frame next to the paragraph so that the top of the frame aligns with the first line of the paragraph. Congratulations. You're done!

No, you're not on drugs; the first line of the typed paragraph will line up with the *bottom* of the drop cap. Framing the drop cap allows you to line it up with the first line of the paragraph (which is how it's supposed to look).

Annotations: An Easy Way for Others to Comment on Your Work

Have you ever sent a copy of a report around for comments and gotten back a bunch of scribbled notes that are difficult to decipher? Well, you can use *annotations* instead. Annotations provide a way for reviewers to add their comments to the document without actually changing it. Annotations are formatted as hidden text so they won't print.

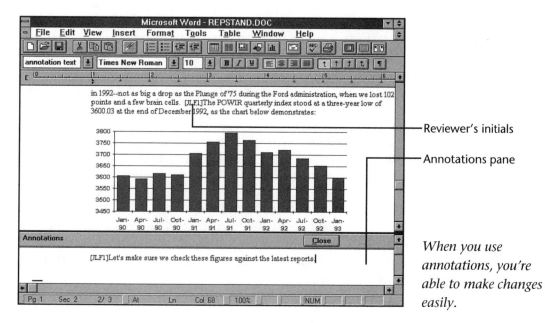

Reviewer's initials

Annotations pane

When you use annotations, you're able to make changes easily.

Before you give your file to your reviewers, lock it for annotations only (so they can't make changes within the document itself). To do so, open the File menu and select the Save As command. Then select File Sharing and the Lock File for Annotations option.

What the Critics Say . . .

A reviewer adds a comment to your file by opening it and moving the insertion point to the place where she would like to add a comment. Next, she opens the Insert menu and selects the Annotation command. The reviewer's initials are inserted into the document, and she types her comments into the Annotation pane (a window that opens at the bottom of the screen). After she finishes entering comments, she clicks on the Close button.

> ### By the Way . . .
>
> If the initials are not set correctly on your reviewer's system, have her open the **Tools** menu and select **Options**. In the Category column, select **User Info**. Have her correct the user initials as necessary and click on **OK**.

To see comments in the file when you get it back, open the View menu and select Annotations. The Annotation pane will open. When you're done reading the comments, click on the Close button. If you need to locate the next annotation, scroll through your document, or open the Edit menu and select Go To. In the Go To box, type **a** (for annotation) and click on **OK**.

You can copy the changes from the Annotation pane into your document by using the **Copy** and **Paste** buttons on the Toolbar. To delete an annotation, select it and press **Delete**.

If you want to print your document and the annotations, open the File menu and select Print. Click on the Options button and under Include with Document use the Annotations check box. If you want to print the annotations only, open the File menu and select Print. Select **Annotations** and click on the **OK** button.

Making Notes to Yourself

Why should your critics have all the fun with annotations? You can add private notes to your document, such as "Remember to update these figures" or "Ask Tom about the new sales report." Using hidden text, these notes will be displayed on-screen but won't print (unless of course you *want to* print them).

To add a secret note, press **Ctrl+H** and type your note. When you're done, press **Ctrl+H** again. To display hidden text, open the Tools menu and select Options. Under Category, select **View** and then check the **Hidden Text** option.

If hidden text is displayed, it affects page numbering, so keep that in mind before you print your document.

If you want to print your notes with your document, open the File menu and select Print. Click on the Options button, and under Include With Document, select Hidden Text.

Read All About It: Creating Your Own Distribution List

If you create documents that need to be routed through several people, you can create a distribution list with boxes that the reader can check off to indicate that she has read the document.

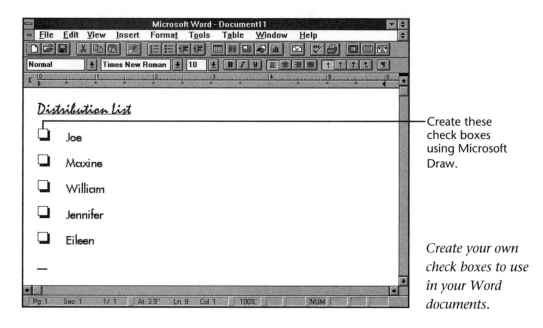

Create these check boxes using Microsoft Draw.

Create your own check boxes to use in your Word documents.

Word for Windows comes with a drawing program, called Microsoft Draw, which you'll be using to create your check boxes. To create a check box, click on the **Draw** button in the Toolbar.

Arrow tool is used to select an object.

White box in front

Rectangle tool

Black box in back

Guidelines

Click here to fill object with black.

You can create your check boxes using Microsoft Draw.

Since we're going to be working on a fairly small object, let's increase the view by opening the View menu and selecting 200% Size. Now click on the **Rectangle** tool and move the mouse pointer to the drawing area. Press the **Shift** key and hold it as you click and drag to create the square for the check box.

Holding the **Shift** key as you drag helps you to create a perfectly square (or round, as the case may be) object.

If you want to create a "shadow" like in the sample, click on your square to select it. Open the Edit menu and select Copy. Open the Edit menu again and select Paste. Select the new square by clicking on it, then click on the black box under Fill at the bottom of the screen.

Now you have a white square and a black square. We'll place the black square behind the white square to create a "shadow." Here's what you do: click on the black square to select it. Drag the black square so that its top right-hand corner is just below and to the right of the top of the white square (use the picture as a guide). If you have trouble moving the two squares precisely, turn on the guidelines by opening the **D**raw menu and selecting Show Guides. We still have one problem: it appears that the black square is on top of the white square. No problem: just open the Edit menu and select **S**end to Back.

When the check box is complete, open the File menu and select Exit and Return. When you're asked if you want to update your document, click on the **Y**es button.

 In your document, select the check box. You can resize it by dragging a corner handle. You can create several copies of the check box by clicking on the **Copy** button and then the **Paste** button.

> **By the Way . . .**
>
> If you want to keep your check box for posterity (and to use in other documents), select it by clicking on it. Open the **E**dit menu and select the Glossary command. Enter a name for the check box, such as "check box," or "shadow box" and click on **D**efine.

When Regular Text Just Isn't Enough

What do you do if you want to enter a date, but you want that date to change whenever you update your document? Well, you use *intelligent fields*. Here are some examples of fields you can insert into your document:

SPEAK LIKE A GEEK

Intelligent field   An intelligent field is text within a document that is automatically updated as changes are made, such as the current date.

- ☛ Current date and time.
- ☛ Name of person who made the last change to this document.
- ☛ Current page number and total number of pages in document.
- ☛ Total number of words and characters in document.
- ☛ Revision number of document.
- ☛ Date the document was last printed.

So how do you get this marvelous feature to work? First, open the Insert menu and select the Field command. In the dialog box that's displayed, scroll through the list until you see the field that you're looking for. Select that field and press **Enter** or click on **OK**.

Font   A font is any set of characters of the same *typeface* (design) and *type size* (measured in points). For example, Times Roman 12-point is a font; Times Roman is the typeface, and 12-point is the size. (There are 72 points in an inch.)

Entering Characters That Aren't on Your Keyboard

Sometimes you may need to enter a character into your document that isn't on your keyboard, such as the cents sign (¢), a trademark (™), the Japanese yen symbol (¥), a tilde (~), or an umlaut (¨). Word makes it super easy to insert strange characters into your document when you need to (or just for fun). Just open the Insert menu and select the Symbol command. In the dialog box that appears, click on any symbol and press **Enter** or click on **OK**.

If you want to browse, open the Symbols From drop-down list box and select a different *font*. If you have a font called Wingdings, try it—the symbols you'll find with that font are as strange as its name.

Putting Your Label on It

You can create customized mailing labels with Word. You'll first have to create your data file (a document that contains the names and addresses of your clients). See Chapter 19 for help.

Once you have your data file created, open a new document by opening the File menu and selecting the New command. In the dialog box, select MAILLABL as your template and then click on **OK**.

A box will appear, asking you to choose between Laser and Dot Matrix. In the next box that appears, choose an Avery Mailing Label type.

Click on either **Single** or **Multiple Labels**. Then, as long as the header record is part of your data file, click on **No**.

Designing Your Mailing Labels

Now it's time to select the fields from your data file to put on the labels:

- ☛ Under Field Names, select a field. Then click on Add to Label.

- ☛ To add a space between fields, or to move to the next line, select that option under Special Characters and click on Add to Label.

- ☛ Repeat for each field. When you're through, click on Done.

Don't forget to add spaces between fields on the same line, such as City, State, and ZIP.

Ready, Set, Print Label!

Word fills a page in your document with the generic fields you selected. You must merge your data file with this document to create your mailing labels.

To print your mailing labels, click on the **Print Merge File** button on the Merge Bar. You can print a range of mailing labels by entering the record numbers under Print Records. Make sure that the **Skip** Completely check box is selected (unless you want to leave a blank line in the middle of a label that contains a blank field, such as a customer with no title).

Save this file by clicking on the **Save** button on the Toolbar. I called mine LABELS. When you want to print labels for this data file again, open this document.

 You can edit the data file by clicking on the Edit Data File button on the Merge Bar before printing the labels again.

The Least You Need to Know

Here's a hodgepodge of the important points in this chapter:

- ☛ To create special effects with text, use MS WordArt.

- ☛ Add a caption to a figure by selecting the figure and pressing **Enter** to create a blank line under the figure.

- ☛ To create a graph, click on the **Graph** button on the Toolbar.

- ☛ To create a drop cap, use MS WordArt to create the letter and put a frame around it so you can place it where you want.

- ☛ Use the Lock File for Annotations option in the **File** Save **As** dialog box to allow others to add comments to your work.

- ☛ To create hidden text, press **Ctrl+H**, type the text, and press **Ctrl+H** again.

- ☛ To create your own check boxes for a distribution list, click on the **Draw** button on the Toolbar.

- ☛ To add a date or other intelligent field to your document, open the Insert menu and select the Field command.

- ☛ To insert a special character into your document, use the **Symbol** command on the Insert menu.

- ☛ To create mailing labels, create a data file, and then open a new document and use the MAILLABL template.

Chapter 23
A Sampling of Word's Document Templates

In This Chapter

- ☛ Writing a business letter
- ☛ Creating a memo or a report
- ☛ Writing a magazine article
- ☛ Sending a fax
- ☛ Writing a dissertation or term paper
- ☛ Printing mailing labels
- ☛ Creating your own overheads
- ☛ Writing a press release or a business proposal

Word has sixteen templates (in addition to the Normal template) that you can use to create documents without all the fuss of selecting margin settings, page orientation, and so on. Most of the templates are automated to make them super easy to use.

To start a document with a Word template, open the File menu and select New. Select the template you want to use and click on **OK**.

By the Way . . .

All the templates include additional commands on the Format menu; look for the Instructions command which provides basic instructions for using each template.

Take a Letter, Please: The Letter Templates

Word offers four different letter templates: Block, Modified Block, Modified Semi-Block, and Personal. When the document opens, you'll be prompted to enter an address. If you've saved the recipient's address as a glossary entry, you can just select it by clicking on the Glossary button. If you need to enter an address, click on the New button.

All the letters provide a place for your name, title, and company. In the Block template (LETBLOCK), all elements (the date, salutation, and closing) are left-aligned. In the Modified Block template (LETMODBK), the date and closing are right-aligned (actually, they are indented about 1/2 inch from the right margin), and the header is a single line that stretches across the top of each page beginning with page two. The Modified Semi-block template (LETMDSEM) features indented paragraphs and right-aligned date and closing. The Personal template (LETPERSN) is less formal than the others and assumes that you don't want to include your title and company name.

By the Way . . .

All the business letters include commands off of the Format menu for creating a fax cover or a mailing label, for changing the letter options (margins, font, salutation, closing, and sender information), and for inserting notations (typist initials, enclosures, attachments, and copy list). You can choose the Create Fax Cover command to create a fax cover for your letter, or use the Create Mailing Label to print a single label.

The Block template.

Mr. Gottried S. Klautchnik
March 7, 1993
Page - 2

Sincerely,

Horace Powell
The Horace Palace

enclosure: Copy of original contract
                Misleading Brochure

The Horace Palace
Your Gateway to the Stars!

March 7, 1993

Mr. Gottried S. Klautchnik
Miscellaneous Other Bookings, Inc.
Behind the Dumpster
Suite B16
Las Vegas, NV 80015

Dear Gottried:

This letter is in regard to one of the entertainers in your employ. Last 21 February, my club, the Horace Palace, booked one of the fellows in your line-up, a person whom your brochure listed as The Amazing Kreskin. I naturally assumed that this Mr. Kreskin of yours would be something of a mind-reader, and would thrill my regular audience with his ability to recall the names and addresses of people he had never met.

I don't recall anyone in your employ having ever told me that this gentleman, a Mr. Elroy Kreskin of Guymon, Oklahoma, had such a way with wresting steers. This also came as a surprise to my clientele of yesterday evening, a Seniors group from the local chapter of Mensa, who were somewhat astounded when rather than guess the contents of ladies' purses, Elroy would juggle them instead. He was, at last, able to guess people's names, though only for people who promised in advance their names began with "Y." "Yvonne? Yvette? Yentl?" he asked one gentleman. When finally one of my guests asked if he could at least demonstrate some prestidigitarianism, Elroy gladly agreed, and proceeded to demonstrate for the audience the proper use of a pocket calculator.

Needless to say, although Elroy is indeed rather talented in certain matters (singing "Oklahoma!" while gargling among them) he is perhaps not quite worth the $15,000 the Horace Palace has paid for the six-week booking. I am requesting a refund, or at least a trade for some other talent for the remainder of the time period. Your brochure lists both The Coasters and Blackstone the Magician; I would be interested in either of these.

If you find it impossible to grant us the refund that we so richly deserve, I will be forced to send all further inquiries to my lawer, Mr. C. Darrow. I do not relish the idea of a long drawn-out court case, but I can assure you that Charlie is not used to losing cases.

Please let me know your intentions by 4:00 tonight. I do not wish to inflict Elroy the singing cowboy on my patrons ever again, so I am quite anxious to resolve this matter. You can reach me at my office, 247-8907, beginning at 8:30 a.m. today.

Mr. Gottried S. Klautchnik   -2-   03/08/93

Sincerely,

Horace Powell

enclosures: Copy of original contract
Misleading brochure

The Horace Palace
Your Gateway to the Stars!

March 8, 1993

Mr. Gottried S. Klautchnik
Miscellaneous Other Bookings, Inc.
Behind the Dumpster
Suite B16
Las Vegas, NV 80015

Dear Gottried,

This letter is in regard to one of the entertainers in your employ. Last 21 February, my club, the Horace Palace, booked one of the fellows in your line-up, a person whom your brochure listed as The Amazing Kreskin. I naturally assumed that this Mr. Kreskin of yours would be something of a mind-reader, and would thrill my regular audience with his ability to recall the names and addresses of people he had never met.

I don't recall anyone in your employ having ever told me that this gentleman, a Mr. Elroy Kreskin of Guymon, Oklahoma, had such a way with wresting steers. This also came as a surprise to my clientele of yesterday evening, a Seniors group from the local chapter of Mensa, who were somewhat astounded when rather than guess the contents of ladies' purses, Elroy would juggle them instead. He was, at last, able to guess people's names, though only for people who promised in advance their names began with "Y." "Yvonne? Yvette? Yentl?" he asked one gentleman. When finally one of my guests asked if he could at least demonstrate some prestidigitarianism, Elroy gladly agreed, and proceeded to demonstrate for the audience the proper use of a pocket calculator.

Needless to say, although Elroy is indeed rather talented in certain matters (singing "Oklahoma!" while gargling among them) he is perhaps not quite worth the $15,000 the Horace Palace has paid for the six-week booking. I am requesting a refund, or at least a trade for some other talent for the remainder of the time period. Your brochure lists both The Coasters and Blackstone the Magician; I would be interested in either of these.

If you find it impossible to grant us the refund that we so richly deserve, I will be forced to send all further inquiries to my lawer, Mr. C. Darrow. I do not relish the idea of a long drawn-out court case, but I can assure you that Charlie is not used to losing cases.

Please let me know your intentions by 4:00 tonight. I do not wish to inflict Elroy the singing cowboy on my patrons ever again, so I am quite anxious to resolve this matter. You can reach me at my office, 247-8907, beginning at 8:30 a.m. today.

The Modified Block template.

Mr. Gottried S. Klautchnik   -2-   03/08/93

                                    Very truly yours,

                                    Horace Powell
                                    The Horace Palace

enclosures: Copy of original contract
                Misleading brochure

*The Modified
Semi-Block template.*

The Horace Palace
Your Gateway to the Stars!

                                                        March 8, 1993

Mr. Gottried S. Klautchnik
Miscellaneous Other Bookings, Inc.
Behind the Dumpster
Suite B16
Las Vegas, NV 80015

Dear Gottried,

     This letter is in regard to one of the entertainers in your employ. Last 21 February, my club, the
Horace Palace, booked one of the fellows in your line-up, a person whom your brochure listed as The
Amazing Kreskin. I naturally assumed that this Mr. Kreskin of yours would be something of a mind-
reader, and would thrill my regular audience with his ability to recall the names and addresses of people
he had never met.

     I don't recall anyone in your employ having ever told me that this gentleman, a Mr. Elroy Kreskin
of Guymon, Oklahoma, had such a way with wresting steers. This also came as a surprise to my clientele
of yesterday evening, a Seniors group from the local chapter of Mensa, who were somewhat astounded
when rather than guess the contents of ladies' purses, Elroy would juggle them instead. He was, at last,
able to guess people's names, though only for people who promised in advance their names began with
"Y." "Yvonne? Yvette? Yentl?" he asked one gentleman. When finally one of my guests asked if he
could at least demonstrate some prestidigitarianism, Elroy gladly agreed, and proceeded to demonstrate
for the audience the proper use of a pocket calculator.

     Needless to say, although Elroy is indeed rather talented in certain matters (singing "Oklahoma!"
while gargling among them) he is perhaps not quite worth the $15,000 the Horace Palace has paid for the
six-week booking. I am requesting a refund, or at least a trade for some other talent for the remainder of
the time period. Your brochure lists both The Coasters and Blackstone the Magician; I would be
interested in either of these.

     If you find it impossible to grant us the refund that we so richly deserve, I will be forced to send all
further inquiries to my lawer, Mr. C. Darrow. I do not relish the idea of a long drawn-out court case, but I
can assure you that Charlie is not used to losing cases.

     Please let me know your intentions by 4:00 tonight. I do not wish to inflict Elroy the singing cowboy
on my patrons ever again, so I am quite anxious to resolve this matter. You can reach me at my office,
247-8907, beginning at 8:30 a.m. today.

Well, if you can't make the Clearwater expedition, maybe you could swing through here on your annual trip to Chicago. You can stay with us; we've added an extra bedroom and we'd love to have you. Give me a ring soon.

Tell Joan I said "Hi!" This template thing seems to be working, so I don't know how much time I'll be able to spend just messing around anymore. It seems that I'm getting pretty good on this thing. Scary, isn't it? Let me know if you can think of a good book to recommend.

Sincerely,

Mark Boyer

5613 E Pithel
San Bernadino, CA 90011

March 7, 1993

Mr. Paul Behrer
5613 E Pithel
San Bernadino, CA 90011

Dear Paul,

It has been a long time since I've written, and for that, I must apologize. Work has been especially hectic lately, what with the move and all. We've installed a computer on everyone's desks now, so I guess I no longer has any excuse not to learn how to use one.

Our company will be using all Windows products. For our word processor, we've chosen Word for Windows, which is partly the reason that you're hearing from me. I've been practicing, and I thought I'd try out the personal letter template and write a letter to you.

Another reason for my writing is that I need help. I've need to get everyone on my staff up and running on Word for Windows, and I was wondering if you could recommend a good tutorial. I'd like something light and entertaining, while being informative.

On to personal matters: Alice and the kids are fine. We went to Clearwater last summer and are planning a return trip this year. Maybe you and Joan would like to join us? It's a fairly low-key kind of town, but it has great beaches, quiet evenings, and interesting local faire.

How's your new job? I heard about your promotion and was wondering how it was going. So you're in charge of 20 people now? Quite a change from our college days when we were hardly in charge of ourselves. Did you picture us as we are now, or did you see a different future in store for the "Cary boys?" Remember old Mr. Finch? I saw him last year and he says "Hello." Still carries that old briefcase -- wonder what he keeps in it. Without his help, I'm not sure that I would have passed chemistry. It was nice to see him again -- he hasn't changed.

What happened to your plans to build a new house? I heard that Joan might be switching jobs and I wondered if that was it. If you could relocate out this way, that would be really cool. I know that Alice would love to spend more time with Joan, and I know that I'd love seeing the two of you more often.

The Personal template.

Magnificent Memos

When you create your first document using the Memo template (MEM02), you'll be prompted to insert a common list of names for distribution. Then you'll need to select the person to whom you are sending a memo, and the names of anyone receiving a courtesy copy.

Use the Set Memo Options command on the Format menu to change the memo title, the margins, or the font. The title, by the way, will print on page two as a header.

By the Way . . .

You can make changes to the distribution list and to the current address by using commands on the Format menu.

InterOffice Memo

To:	Billy Bob Mullins
From:	Heinrich Glich, COMO
Date:	March 8, 1993
Subject:	Testing this Memo Template

This memo has been written and conceived by me in an attempt to see how this memo-writing template works. Please be advised that this memo-writing template works fine.

Speaking of memos, in the future, I would like to see from you less doing and more *thinking*! Thinking, my boy, is the key to this business. The phrase, after all, is not , "I *do* therefore I am!" So you must think before you *do*. From now on That's an order (TAO).

CC: Robert C. Arnett, Doris Hutchit

The Memo template.

Landscape orientation   Your document is oriented so that it is wider than it is long, as in 11" x 8 1/2". The opposite of landscape orientation is portrait.

Portrait orientation   Your document is oriented so that it is longer than it is wide, as in 8 1/2" x 11". This is the normal orientation of most documents. The opposite of portrait orientation is landscape.

As You Can See, on Page 23: The Report Templates

Word offers three different report templates: a report in portrait orientation, a report in landscape orientation, and a report with side headings.

When you open a report template, it will ask you for basic information, such as your company's name, your name, your title, and the report's title (and subtitle), that it uses to create the report's own title page. Section headings (heading 1 style) and subheadings (heading 2 style) are placed in the document as dummies; just type over them with your own heading titles or delete the ones you don't want. The footer includes the report's title, the page number, and the closest title using the heading 1 style.

The Standard report (REPSTAND) features left-aligned headings and paragraphs that are indented (all lines) from the left. The Landscape report (REPLAND) is the same, but it's printed so that the paper is wider than it is long (for example, 11" x 8 1/2"). The report with side headings (REPSIDE) has a two column format that places headings left-aligned within the left-hand column.

By the Way . . .

Commands that you'll encounter on the Format menu include Set Report Options (for changing the title, etc.), Insert New Section (for adding a new section to the report; it starts with two dummy sections in place), Change Fonts (for changing the report font), and Create Fax Cover (now what could that be for?).

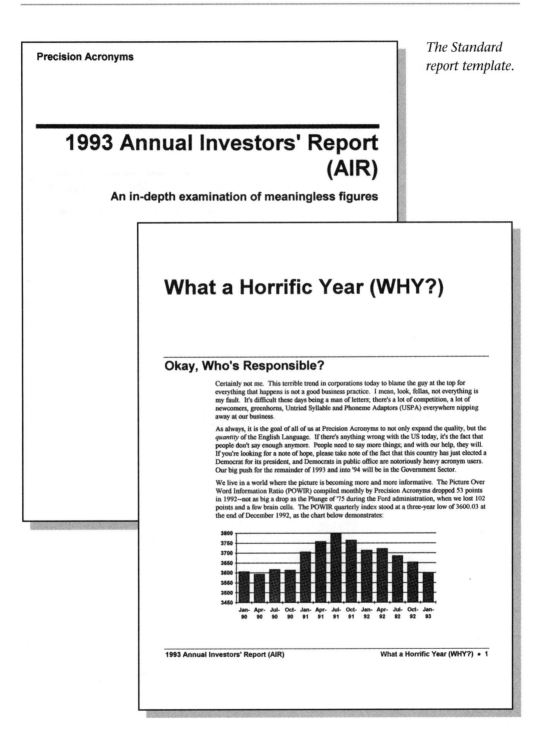

The Standard report template.

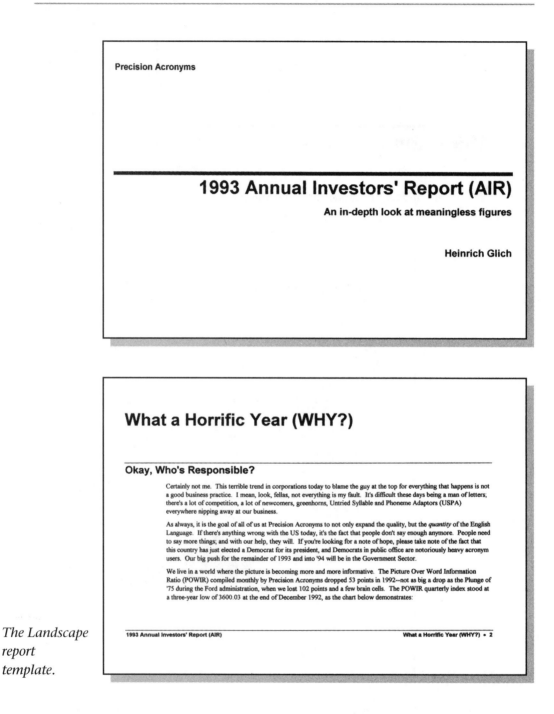

Precision Acronyms

1993 Annual Investors' Report (AIR)

An in-depth look at meaningless figures

Heinrich Glich

What a Horrific Year (WHY?)

Okay, Who's Responsible?

Certainly not me. This terrible trend in corporations today to blame the guy at the top for everything that happens is not a good business practice. I mean, look, fellas, not everything is my fault. It's difficult these days being a man of letters; there's a lot of competition, a lot of newcomers, greenhorns, Untried Syllable and Phoneme Adaptors (USPA) everywhere nipping away at our business.

As always, it is the goal of all of us at Precision Acronyms to not only expand the quality, but the *quantity* of the English Language. If there's anything wrong with the US today, it's the fact that people don't say enough anymore. People need to say more things; and with our help, they will. If you're looking for a note of hope, please take note of the fact that this country has just elected a Democrat for its president, and Democrats in public office are notoriously heavy acronym users. Our big push for the remainder of 1993 and into '94 will be in the Government Sector.

We live in a world where the picture is becoming more and more informative. The Picture Over Word Information Ratio (POWIR) compiled monthly by Precision Acronyms dropped 53 points in 1992--not as big a drop as the Plunge of '75 during the Ford administration, when we lost 102 points and a few brain cells. The POWIR quarterly index stood at a three-year low of 3600.03 at the end of December 1992, as the chart below demonstrates:

1993 Annual Investors' Report (AIR)   What a Horrific Year (WHY?) • 2

The Landscape report template.

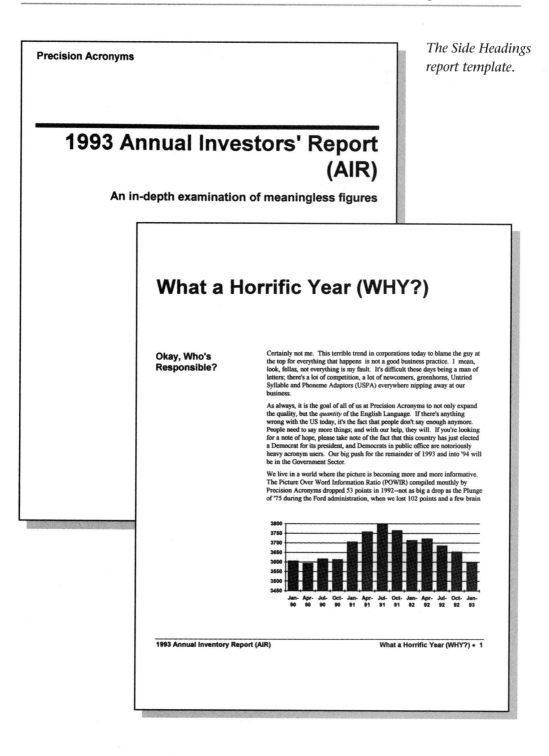

Precision Acronyms

1993 Annual Investors' Report (AIR)

An in-depth examination of meaningless figures

What a Horrific Year (WHY?)

Okay, Who's Responsible?

Certainly not me. This terrible trend in corporations today to blame the guy at the top for everything that happens is not a good business practice. I mean, look, fellas, not everything is my fault. It's difficult these days being a man of letters; there's a lot of competition, a lot of newcomers, greenhorns, Untried Syllable and Phoneme Adaptors (USPA) everywhere nipping away at our business.

As always, it is the goal of all of us at Precision Acronyms to not only expand the quality, but the *quantity* of the English Language. If there's anything wrong with the US today, it's the fact that people don't say enough anymore. People need to say more things; and with our help, they will. If you're looking for a note of hope, please take note of the fact that this country has just elected a Democrat for its president, and Democrats in public office are notoriously heavy acronym users. Our big push for the remainder of 1993 and into '94 will be in the Government Sector.

We live in a world where the picture is becoming more and more informative. The Picture Over Word Information Ratio (POWIR) compiled monthly by Precision Acronyms dropped 53 points in 1992--not as big a drop as the Plunge of '75 during the Ford administration, when we lost 102 points and a few brain

Submitted for Your Approval: The Article Template

Use the Article template to create magazine articles. This template follows the guidelines described in the *Writer's Market 1991*.

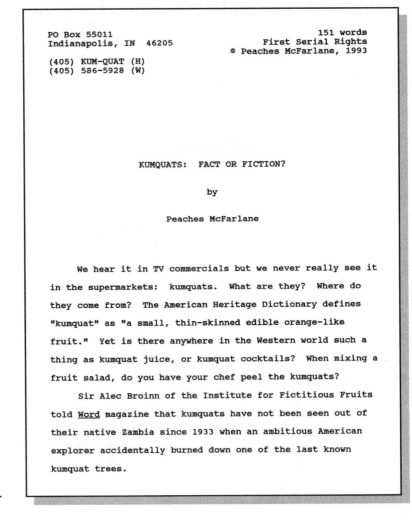

PO Box 55011
Indianapolis, IN 46205

(405) KUM-QUAT (H)
(405) 586-5928 (W)

151 words
First Serial Rights
© Peaches McFarlane, 1993

KUMQUATS: FACT OR FICTION?

by

Peaches McFarlane

We hear it in TV commercials but we never really see it
in the supermarkets: kumquats. What are they? Where do
they come from? The American Heritage Dictionary defines
"kumquat" as "a small, thin-skinned edible orange-like
fruit." Yet is there anywhere in the Western world such a
thing as kumquat juice, or kumquat cocktails? When mixing a
fruit salad, do you have your chef peel the kumquats?

Sir Alec Broinn of the Institute for Fictitious Fruits
told Word magazine that kumquats have not been seen out of
their native Zambia since 1933 when an ambitious American
explorer accidentally burned down one of the last known
kumquat trees.

The Article template.

When you open a document with this template (ARTICLE2), you'll be asked for a title, your name, address, and phone numbers, your social security number, and the type of publishing rights you are offering.

> ### By the Way . . .
> There are two commands on the Format menu that you might use: Set Article Options (which allows you to change the title and contact information) and Create Fax Cover (which allows you to create a fax cover using the Fax template—see the next section).

Just the Fax, Ma'am

The Fax template (FAX) can be used to create a cover sheet for anything you send over a fax. The Fax template is activated via a command on the Format menu from within other templates, such as the Article template.

When you create a new document using the Fax template, you'll be prompted for information on the person you're sending the fax to and the number of pages to be sent.

> ### By the Way . . .
> On the Format menu, you'll find the command Change Fax Defaults, which allows you to change the name and phone numbers of the person sending the fax.

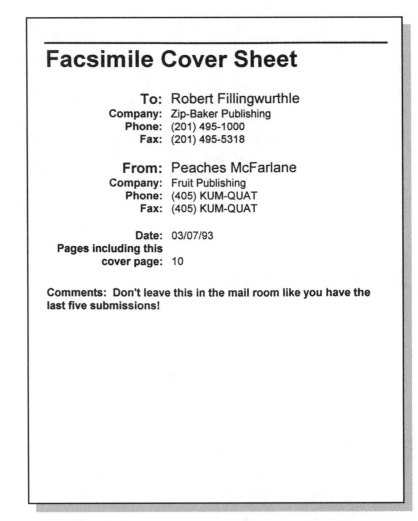

Facsimile Cover Sheet

To: Robert Fillingwurthle
Company: Zip-Baker Publishing
Phone: (201) 495-1000
Fax: (201) 495-5318

From: Peaches McFarlane
Company: Fruit Publishing
Phone: (405) KUM-QUAT
Fax: (405) KUM-QUAT

Date: 03/07/93
Pages including this cover page: 10

Comments: Don't leave this in the mail room like you have the last five submissions!

The Fax template.

The Effects of Boredom While Writing Dissertations

If you've ever written a dissertation, you know how exacting a process it can be. The Dissertation template (DISSERT2) takes some of the pain out of writing dissertations because it's based on the guide *A Manual for Writers of Term Papers, Theses, and Dissertations, 5th ed.*

ACKNOWLEDGMENTS

I would like to thank my parents for having me, and my
roommate Steve for loaning me his computer, and for teaching
me how to use Word for Windows. I would also like to thank
the author of this great book, "The Complete Idiot's Guide
to Word for Windows," who must be a really gifted and
talented person.

The Dissertation template.

OKLAHOMA INSTITUTE OF SCIENCE AND FOOTBALL

THE ELONGATED EFFECTS OF FOOTBALL ON THE ETHIOPIAN BARN SWALLOW

A DISSERTATION SUBMITTED TO

THE FACULTY OF THE DIVISION OF ETHICAL, MORAL, AND SPORTSMANLIKE
SCIENCES

IN CANDIDACY FOR THE DEGREE OF DOCTOR OF ADVANCED TEMPLATE USAGE

DEPARTMENT OF THINKOLOGY

BY

WALLY FIGG

PONOTOC, OKLAHOMA

MARCH, 1993

You'll need to use the Insert **D**issertation Part command to insert each and every part of your dissertation.

Use the Insert **D**issertation Part command on the Forma**t** menu to insert any part of your dissertation. For example, move to the beginning of the document and choose **Title**, and you'll be prompted for the title, your name, and information about the university to which you're submitting this dissertation.

Be sure to open and print the TEMPLATE.DOC which is located in the WORD directory. It contains detailed information on how to use this template.

Almost as Boring: Writing a Term Paper

Well, at least writing a term paper is easier when you use the Term Paper template (TERM2). Like the Dissertation template, the style for this template is based on *A Manual for Writers of Term Papers, Theses, and Dissertations, 5th ed.*

By the Way . . .

There are several commands on the Forma**t** menu for inserting each part of your term paper. For example, move to the beginning of the document and choose Insert Title **P**age, and you'll be prompted for the title, your name, and the date. Like the Dissertation template, you should open and print TEMPLATE.DOC for more information before using this template.

BARBARA GARTLAND AND HERMAN MELVILLE: DIFFERENCES AND
SIMILARITIES

BY
HEIDI ARDENWEEDLE
MARCH 8, 1993

"Call me Ishmael." So begins the third greatest novel
in the history of novels, the famous <u>Moby Dick</u> by the famous
Herman Melville. But think about it. How many copies of
<u>Moby Dick</u> were sold in its first five weeks? Surely not as
many as <u>Awakening Lands</u> or <u>Bright Glows the Beacon</u> or
<u>Wherefore Art Thou, Heinrich?</u> by the famous romance
novelist, Barbara Gartland.

Did Herman Melville ever write of love or honor or the
tragedy of personal loss? No, he wrote about this guy with
a wooden leg, and about this huge whale, and about this
weird thing called "cetology." Who cares about whales in
this modern world? Whales are old. People today want to
read about love, and loving more than one person, and people
who have more than three lovers, and people who got divorced

The Term Paper template.

Look Fo-o-or the Mailing Lab-el

You can print mailing labels for standard Avery labels by using the Mailing Labels template (MAILLABL). You can enter your own addresses or bring them in from a data file (see merging in Chapter 19 for more information).

The letter templates, such as the Block template, offer a command to create a single mailing label for the current letter. Look for it under the Format menu.

Maurice Van Gough
Petrol Chemicals, Inc.
PO Box 15441
Jeddah 21444,   Saudi Arabia

Stephen P. Kyle

1556 California Court
Apartment #5
Mountain Pass, CA 94041

Roberta S. Blake

1027 Coleturn Road
Columbus, OH 43219

John Quigley
John P. Quigley & Associates
5660 Kirby Ave.
Suite 1950
Houston, TX 77005

Mary Lou Minor
Radical Information Systems
358 Pettry Circle
Macon, GA 31204

Alice A. Nagley

1239 Pilgrim Lane
Friendswood, TX 77546

Sally Pikowsky
The Dorix Ink Company
1023 Broadway
Suite 122233
Oakland, CA 94607

Robert Taylor
Rich Pintel Inc.
25358 Avenue Stestley
Valencia, CA 91355

John Blue
Tippen Hydraulics Corp.
1312 University Parkway
Sarasota, FA 34243

Marcos Ilianna

70 Washington Street
Perth Amboy, NJ 08661

Gloria DeHaven
GLF Software
1445 Springhouse Lane
Media, PA 19063-5231

Edward T. Smithson
Timely Solutions
52 Plowridge Road
Levittown, PA 19056-1122

The Mailing Labels template.

Can Everyone See? Using the Overhead Template

The easiest way to create professional-looking overheads is to start with the Overhead template (OVERHEAD). When you create a document with this template, you'll be prompted for information for your title page. After the title page, space for the first transparency is inserted. To insert additional slides (transparencies) use the Insert New Slide command on the Format menu.

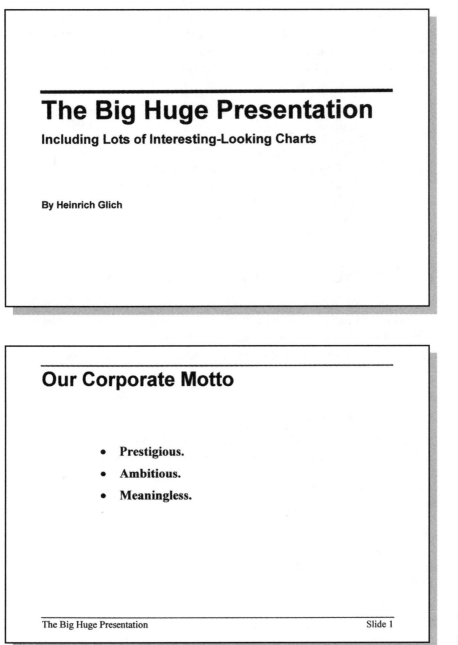

The Overhead template.

There are three styles that you should use while creating your slides: Heading 1 (for the title of each slide), and Heading 2 and 3 (for bulleted items). If you originally used numbered lists and you want to convert them to bullets, use the Apply Bullets command on the Format menu.

By the Way . . .

There are additional commands on the Format menu: Update Title Page, Change Fonts, and Create Fax Cover. If you need to change the order of your slides, switch to Outline view.

Hold the Presses, It's a Press Release!

When you open a new document with the Press Release template (PRESS), you'll be prompted for a headline which will be used for a header beginning on page two. You'll also be prompted for contact information. The template follows the style described in the *Associated Press Stylebook*.

By the Way . . .

There are two commands on the Format menu: Create Fax Cover (pretty standard among all the business-related templates) and Update Press Release Info (which allows you to change the title and contact info).

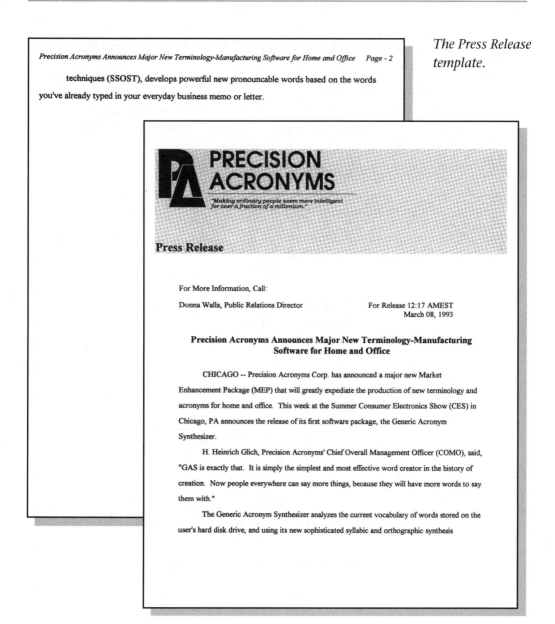

The Press Release template.

May I Make a Suggestion? Writing Proposals

When you open a new document with the Proposal template (PROPOSAL), you'll be prompted for a title, along with submitted by/to information. All three of these will appear not only on the title page, but in headers for subsequent pages. You can of course change any of these with the Update Title Information command on the Format menu.

As you create your proposal, use the Heading 1 style for the major points; they will appear with a top border which sets off their section. Within each section, use the Heading 2 and 3 styles for subsections.

H. Heinrich Glich, COMO

Proposal to Write Infinitely More Proposals (WIMP)
Submitted to:
Submitted by: Collette Morgan, CPO

Proposal to Write Infinitely More Proposals (WIMP)

Why Do It?

As part of this year's Prestigious/Ambitious/Meaningless advertising campaign, to project an attitude within the company of inherent busy-ness, we should think of more things to think of. That is to say, not necessarily *do*, but as long as it appears, even to us, that we're thinking of something important to do, or say, or even to think, then I think we're doing more.

Keep On Proposin'

Internal studies made by our Business Internal Studies (BIS) division show that time spent proposing new ideas in planning meanings consumes not only valuable time but valuable energy. Since consumption, the decree of our founder, H. Hermann Glich once wrote, is our ultimate goal, then we should indeed investigate new ways to spend time and energy. Therefore I propose that we have the Overall Bureaucracy division form a Special Proposal Investigative Team (SPIT) to work out new and innovative ways to think of things to say during meetings.

Impressive Things to Say to Fill Space

It will be the goal of SPIT to devise new methods for the creation and mass-production of proposals and cost estimates. Agencies of the Federal Government are already hard at work, meeting with the acting representatives of SPIT, working out timetables for visits by members of Congress. These officials will oversee the things we do here, and hopefully will emulate our activities in Washington.

Stage One: Government Involvement (SOGI)

It is of prime importance that we enlist the aid of the Federal Government in these affairs. First of all, we are in the business of manufacturing a product that they consume in mass quantities. No, not that. . . I'm referring to *non-words*. Our primary customer, the Defense Advanced Research Projects Agency (DARPA) uses our technology every day to devise new and

Page 1

The Proposal template.

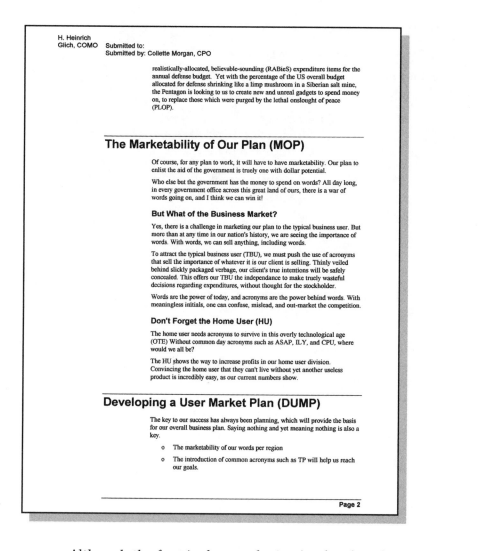

H. Heinrich
Glich, COMO   Submitted to:
              Submitted by: Collette Morgan, CPO

realistically-allocated, believable-sounding (RABieS) expenditure items for the annual defense budget. Yet with the percentage of the US overall budget allocated for defense shrinking like a limp mushroom in a Siberian salt mine, the Pentagon is looking to us to create new and unreal gadgets to spend money on, to replace those which were purged by the lethal onslought of peace (PLOP).

The Marketability of Our Plan (MOP)

Of course, for any plan to work, it will have to have marketability. Our plan to enlist the aid of the government is truely one with dollar potential.

Who else but the government has the money to spend on words? All day long, in every government office across this great land of ours, there is a war of words going on, and I think we can win it!

But What of the Business Market?

Yes, there is a challenge in marketing our plan to the typical business user. But more than at any time in our nation's history, we are seeing the importance of words. With words, we can sell anything, including words.

To attract the typical business user (TBU), we must push the use of acronyms that sell the importance of whatever it is our client is selling. Thinly veiled behind slickly packaged verbage, our client's true intentions will be safely concealed. This offers our TBU the independance to make truely wasteful decisions regarding expenditures, without thought for the stockholder.

Words are the power of today, and acronyms are the power behind words. With meaningless initials, one can confuse, mislead, and out-market the competition.

Don't Forget the Home User (HU)

The home user needs acronyms to survive in this overly technological age (OTE) Without common day acronyms such as ASAP, ILY, and CPU, where would we all be?

The HU shows the way to increase profits in our home user division. Convincing the home user that they can't live without yet another useless product is incredibly easy, as our current numbers show.

Developing a User Market Plan (DUMP)

The key to our success has always been planning, which will provide the basis for our overall business plan. Saying nothing and yet meaning nothing is also a key.

o   The marketability of our words per region

o   The introduction of common acronyms such as TP will help us reach our goals.

Page 2

Although the font is clean and crisp (perfect for a business proposal), you can change it with the Change Fonts command on the Format menu.

The Least You Need to Know

Let me fill in the blanks on what was important in this chapter:

- ☞ To start a new document with a particular template, open the **File** menu and select **O**pen. Then under Template, select the template you want to use.

- ☞ Switch the template you're using by opening the **File** menu and selecting the **T**emplate command.

- ☞ Look for additional commands with each template on the Format menu.

Well, looking at the old clock on the wall, I see that I'm about out of paper. Thanks for hanging in there . . .

If you need help installing Word for Windows (yeah, I know, now I tell you) or if you aren't sure what a particular word means, check out the installation page or the glossary.

Speak Like a Geek: The Complete Archive

The computer world is like an exclusive club complete with its own language. If you want to be accepted, you need to learn the lingo (the secret handshake will come later). The following mini-glossary will help you get started.

accelerator keys   (1) The one thing you don't want to be pressing when you see a cop. (2) Sometimes called shortcut keys, these are used to activate a command without opening the menu. Usually a function key or a key combination, such as Alt+F12, accelerator keys are displayed next to the menu command. To use an accelerator key, hold down the first key while you press the second key.

active document   The document you are currently working in. The active document contains the insertion point, and if more than one document window is being displayed on-screen, the active document's title bar appears darker than the other title bars.

alignment   Controls how the text in a paragraph is placed between the left and right margins. For example, you might have left-aligned or centered text.

application   (1) The placement of shampoo on the head. (2) Also known as a *program*, a set of instructions that enable a computer to perform a specific task, such as word processing or data management.

ASCII file   A file containing characters that can be used by any program on any computer. Sometimes called a *text file* or an *ASCII text file*. (ASCII is pronounced "ASK-key.")

boilerplate text   Generic text within a template that is reused by every document created from that template. For example, "Dear Valued Customer" and "Sincerely Yours" qualify as boilerplate text for a form letter.

border   A line placed on any (or all) of the four sides of a block of text, a graphic, a chart, or a table.

bulleted list   Similar to a numbered list. A bulleted list is a series of paragraphs with hanging indents, where the bullet (usually a dot or a check mark) is placed to the left of all the other lines in the paragraph. A bulleted list is often used to display a list of items or to summarize important points.

cell   (1) The opposite of "Buy!" (2) The box formed by the intersection of a row and a column in a Word table. The same term is used when describing the intersection of a row and a column in a spreadsheet. A cell may contain text, a numeric value, or a formula.

click   To move the mouse pointer over an object or icon and press and release the mouse button once without moving the mouse.

clip art   A collection of prepackaged artwork whose individual pieces can be placed within a document.

Clipboard   (1) A wooden or plastic rectangle to which you can affix important notes so you can lose them for a week after the wooden or plastic rectangle accidentally falls behind your filing cabinet. (2) A temporary storage area that holds text and graphics. The cut and copy commands put text or graphics on the Clipboard, erasing the Clipboard's previous contents. The paste command copies Clipboard data to a document.

columns   A vertical section of a table. See also *newspaper-style columns*.

command   An order that tells the computer what to do. In command-driven programs, you have to press a specific key or type the command to execute it. With menu-driven programs, you select the command from a menu.

computer   (1) A hole on my desk I throw money into. (2) Any machine that accepts input (from a user), processes the input, and produces output in some form.

Control-menu box   A special button located in the upper left corner of a window that contains a special menu that can be used to move, size, and close a window with the keyboard.

crash   (1) A sound you don't want to hear when you're moving your computer. (2) Failure of a system or program. Usually, you will realize that your system crashed when the display or keyboard locks up. The term *crash* also refers to a disk crash or head crash, which occurs when the read/write head in the disk drive falls on the disk. This would be like dropping a phonograph needle on a record. A disk crash can destroy any data stored where the read/write head fell on the disk.

cropping   The process of cutting away part of an imported graphic.

cursor   A horizontal line that appears below characters. A cursor acts like the tip of your pencil; anything you type appears at the cursor. (See also *insertion point.*)

data   (1) That guy on *Star Trek: The Next Generation.* (2) A computer term for information. You enter facts and figures (data) into a computer, which then processes it and displays it in an organized manner. In common usage, *data* and *information* are used interchangeably.

data files   A special document file that contains the variable information that is later merged with a main document to produce individual form letters or mailing labels.

database   A type of computer program used for storing, organizing, and retrieving information. Popular database programs include Microsoft Access, dBASE, Paradox, and Q&A.

desktop publishing (DTP)   A program that allows you to combine text and graphics on the same page and manipulate the text and the graphics on-screen. Desktop publishing programs are commonly used to create newsletters, brochures, flyers, resumes, and business cards.

dialog box   (1) Geek name for a telephone. (2) A special window or box that appears when the program requires additional information before executing a command.

directory   Because large hard disks can store thousands of files, you often need to store related files in separate directories on the disk. Think of your disk as a filing cabinet and think of each directory as a drawer in the filing cabinet. By keeping files in separate directories, it is easier to locate and work with related files.

disk   A round, flat, magnetic storage unit. See *floppy disks* and *hard disk*.

disk drive   (1) A street in Silicon Valley. (2) A device that writes and reads data on a magnetic disk. Think of a disk drive as being like a cassette recorder/player. Just as the cassette player can record sounds on a magnetic cassette tape and play back those sounds, a disk drive can record data on a magnetic disk and play back that data.

document   Any work you create using an application program and save in a file on disk. Although the term *document* traditionally refers to work created in a word processing program, such as a letter or a chapter of a book, *document* is now loosely used to refer to any work, including spreadsheets and databases.

document window   A window which frames the controls and information for the document file being worked on. You can have multiple document windows open at one time.

DOS (disk operating system)   DOS, which rhymes with "boss," is an essential program that provides the instructions necessary for the computer's parts (keyboard, disk drive, central processing unit, display screen, printer, and so on) to function as a unit.

DOS prompt   An on-screen prompt that indicates DOS is ready to accept a command. It looks something like C> or C:\>.

double-click   To move the mouse pointer over an object or icon and press and release the mouse button twice in quick succession.

drag   (1) Losing a winning lottery ticket. (2) To drag the mouse, first move the mouse to the starting position. Now click and hold the left mouse button. Drag the mouse to the ending position, and then release the mouse button.

drop cap A *drop cap* (or dropped capital as Word calls it) is used to set off the first letter in a paragraph. The letter is enlarged and set into the text of the paragraph, at its upper left-hand corner.

edit To make changes to existing information. Editing in a word processor usually involves spell-checking, grammar checking, and making formatting changes until the document is judged to be complete.

embedded object An object that maintains a connection to the application that created it, so that if changes are needed, you can access that application by double-clicking on the object. An embedded object is stored within your Word document.

end mark A way of marking the end of the document; as you enter text, this mark will move down.

extension In DOS, each file you create has a unique name. The name consists of two parts: a file name and an extension. The file name can be up to eight characters. The extension (which is optional) can be up to three characters. The extension normally denotes the file type.

facing pages An option you can use when creating magazine-like reports: when open, the pages of your report would "face each other."

field (1) What someone is always out standing in. (2) One part of a data file *record*. A field contains a single piece of information (for example, a telephone number, ZIP code, or a person's last name).

file (1) What every prisoner wants to find in their birthday cake. (2) DOS stores information in files. Anything can be placed in a file: a memo, a budget report, or even a graphics image (like a picture of a boat or a computer). Each document you create in Word for Windows is stored in its own file. Files always have a file name to identify them.

fixed disk drive A disk drive that has a non-removable disk, as opposed to floppy drives, in which you can insert and remove disks. See also *disk drive*.

floppy disk drive A disk drive that uses floppy disks. See also *disk drive*.

floppy disks   Small, portable, plastic storage squares that magnetically store *data* (the facts and figures you enter and save). Floppy disks are inserted into your computer's *floppy disk drive* (located on the front of the computer).

font   Any set of characters which share the same *typeface* (style or design). Fonts convey the mood and style of a document. Technically, font describes the combination of the *typeface* and the *point size* of a character, as in Times Roman 12-point, but in common usage it describes only a character's style or typeface.

footer   (1) The distance my golf ball travels when I tee off. (2) Text that can be repeated at the bottom of every page within a document.

formatting   The process of changing the look of a character (by making it bold, underlined, and slightly bigger, for example) or a paragraph (by centering the paragraph between the margins or by adding an automatic indentation for the first line, for example).

frames   Small boxes in which you place text or pictures so you can easily maneuver them within your document.

function keys   The 10 or 12 F keys on the left side of the keyboard or 12 F keys at the top of the keyboard. F keys are numbered F1, F2, F3, and so on. These keys are used to enter various commands in the Word program.

glossary   (1) A type of house paint which is the opposite of flattery. (2) A part of Word where you can store commonly used text and graphics. Using a glossary saves you the trouble of typing repetitious phrases (such as a greeting and salutation) in every document.

Grammar Checker   A special program within Word for Windows that corrects errors of a grammatical nature within a document.

graphic   A picture which can be imported into Word in order to illustrate a particular point.

graphical user interface (GUI, pronounced gooey)   (1) Tar on a hot tin roof. (2) A type of program interface that uses graphical elements, such as icons, to represent commands, files, and (in some cases) other programs. The most popular GUI is Microsoft Windows.

graphics/charting program   A program (such as Microsoft Graph) that takes columnar data and creates a professional-looking chart.

gutter   (1) A leaf, twig, and debris magnet. (2) An unused region of space that runs down the inside edges of facing pages of a document; it's the part of each page that is used when the pages of a book or a magazine are bound together.

handles   Small black squares that surround a graphic or frame after it is selected.

hanging indent   A special kind of indent where the first line of a paragraph hangs closer to the left margin than the rest of the lines in the paragraph. Typically used for bulleted or numbered lists.

hard disk   A nonremoveable disk drive that stores many megabytes of data. Because it is fixed inside the computer (see *fixed disk drive*), it performs quicker and more efficiently than a floppy disk.

hardware   The physical parts of a computer (such as the *monitor*, the *disk drives*, the *CPU*, and so on). The programs you run are electronic, rather than physical; they're known as *software*.

header   Text that can be repeated at the top of every page within a document.

header record   Stores the field names (column headings) for a data file.

icon   A graphic image that represents another object, such as a program.

indent   The amount of distance from the page margins to the edges of your paragraph.

input   Data that goes into your computer. When you press a key or click a mouse button, you are giving your computer input. Data that your computer gives back to you (by printing it out or displaying it on the monitor) is called *output*.

Insert mode   The default typing mode for most word processors and text editors. Insert mode means that when you position your cursor and start to type, what you type is inserted at that point, and existing text is pushed to the right.

insertion point   A blinking vertical line used in some word processors to indicate the place where any characters you type will be inserted. An insertion point is the equivalent of a *cursor.*

intelligent field   Text within a Word document that is automatically updated as changes are made (for example, a date field that updates whenever a document is changed).

jump term   A highlighted term in the Word for Windows help system that, when selected, "jumps" to a related section of the help system.

keyboard   The main input device for most computers.

kilobyte   A unit for measuring the amount of data. A kilobyte (K) is equivalent to 1,024 bytes.

landscape orientation   Your document is oriented so that it is wider than it is long, as in 11" x 8 1/2". The opposite of landscape orientation is portrait.

leader   (1) Someone that aliens are always asking to be taken to. (2) Dots or dashes that fill the spaces between tab positions in a columnar list.

linked object   An imported object (such as a graphic) that maintains a connection to the program that created it, so that if changes are made to that object, those changes can be updated (either automatically or through a command) into your document. A linked object is stored separately from your Word document.

macro   A recorded set of instructions for a frequently used task, which can be activated by pressing a specified key combination. Macros resemble small programs.

margin   An area on the left, right, top, and bottom sides of a page that is usually left blank. Text flows between the margins of a page.

Maximize button   An upward pointing arrow located in the upper right-hand corner of a window that, when clicked on, causes that window to fill the screen.

megabyte   A standard unit used to measure the storage capacity of a disk and the amount of computer memory. A megabyte is 1,048,576 bytes (1000 kilobytes). This is roughly equivalent to 500 pages of double-spaced text. Megabyte is commonly abbreviated as M, MB, or Mbyte.

memory   Electronic storage area inside the computer, used to temporarily store data or program instructions when the computer is using them. The computer's memory is erased when the power to the computer is turned off.

menu   A list of commands or instructions displayed on the screen. Menus organize commands and make a program easier to use.

menu bar   Located at the top of the Program Window, this displays a list of menus which contain the commands you'll use to edit documents.

merging   The process of combining variable information stored in a *data file* with a *main document* in order to produce a series of form letters or mailing labels.

Microsoft   (1)A company I wish I had lots of stock in. (2)The company that brought you Word for Windows, Microsoft Graph, Microsoft Draw, Microsoft Equation Editor, and (among others) Windows itself.

Minimize button   A downward pointing arrow located in the upper right-hand corner of a window that, when clicked on, causes that window to be reduced to an icon on your screen.

monitor   A television-like screen that lets the computer display information.

mouse   (1) The last name of a little guy named Mickey. (2) A device that moves an arrow (a pointer) around the screen. When you move the mouse, the pointer on the screen moves in the same direction. Used instead of the keyboard to select and move items (such as text or graphics), execute commands, and perform other tasks. A mouse gets its name because it connects to your computer through a long "tail" or cord.

mouse pad   (1) Where Mickey and his friends hang out. (2) A small square of plastic or foam that the mouse rests on. A mouse pad provides better traction for the mouse, while keeping it away from dust and other goop on your desk.

MS-DOS (Microsoft Disk Operating System)   See *DOS.*

newspaper-style columns   Similar to the style of column found in newspapers. Text in these columns flows between invisible boundaries down one part of the page. At the end of the page, the text continues at the top of the next column. Columns can be "interrupted" by graphics (pictures or charts) that illustrate the story being told.

numbered list   Similar to a bulleted list. A numbered list is a series of paragraphs with hanging indents, where the number is placed to the left of all the other lines in the paragraph. Used in numbering the steps for a procedure.

output   Data (computer information) that your computer gives back to you. Output can be displayed on a computer's monitor, stored on disk, or printed on the printer. Output is the opposite of *input*, which is the data that you enter into the computer.

Overtype mode   The opposite of *Insert mode*, as used in word processors and text editors. Overtype mode means that when you position your cursor and start to type, what you type replaces existing characters at that point.

page break   A dotted line which marks the end of a page. A page break can be forced within a document by pressing Ctrl+Enter.

pane   (1) What I feel when someone touches my shoulder after I've spent all day at the beach. (2) What Word for Windows calls the special boxes that you use when adding headers, footers, footnotes, and annotations. In Normal View, a pane appears in the bottom half of the document window. (Since it's part of a window—rather than being a separate box like a dialog box—it's called a pane.)

paragraph   Any grouping of words that should be treated as a unit. This includes normal paragraphs as well as single-line paragraphs, such as chapter titles, section headings, and captions for charts or other figures. When you press Enter/Return in Word for Windows, you are marking the end of a paragraph.

parallel columns   See *table*.

passive voice   (1) Speaking in a whisper. (2) A type of sentence that states what is done to the subject, rather than what the subject is doing (for example, "The race was won by Mary Ann"). Active voice (as in "Mary Ann won the race") is the opposite of passive voice.

PC   See *personal computer*.

pie chart   A type of chart shaped like a circle, which is divided into pieces, like a pie. Each item that's charted (such as AT&T, MCI, and Sprint) is given a "pie piece" which represents their portion of the whole circle.

point   To move the mouse pointer so that it is on top of a specific object on the screen.

point size   The type size of a particular character. There are 72 points in an inch. Font families usually have only certain point sizes available; if you need larger or smaller letters than your font offers, switch to a different font.

portrait orientation   Your document is oriented so that it is longer than it is wide, as in 8 1/2" x 11". This is the normal orientation of most documents. The opposite of portrait orientation is landscape.

printer   Most computers have a printer for printing copies of data. The data that comes out of your computer is called *output*.

program   A group of instructions written in a special "machine language" which the computer understands. Typical programs are word processors, spreadsheets, databases, and games.

program group   A special window within the Program Manager that is used to group several applications together. In the Word for Windows program group, you will find two icons: Word and Word Setup.

program window   The window that Word for Windows runs in. Close this window, and you close down (exit) Word for Windows. This window frames the tools and the menus for the Word for Windows program.

pull-down menu   A *pull-down* menu contains the selections for a main menu command. This type of menu, when activated, is pulled down below the main menu bar, like a window shade can be pulled down from the top of a window frame.

random-access memory (RAM)   What your computer uses to temporarily store data and programs. RAM is measured in kilobytes and megabytes. Generally the more RAM a computer has, the more powerful programs it can run.

readability index   A measure of the education level a reader would need to easily understand the text in a given document. It is determined by counting the average number of words per sentence and the average number of syllables per 100 words. (A good average is about 17 words per sentence and 147 syllables per 100 words.)

rebooting   The process of restarting a computer that is already on. Press **Ctrl+Alt+Delete** to reboot. Also known as *warm booting*.

record   In a data file, this denotes a collection of related information contained in one or more fields, such as an individual's name, address, and phone number. A record is stored in a single row of a Word data file.

Restore button   A special double-headed arrow located in the upper right-hand corner of a window that, when clicked on, restores a window to its previous size.

Ribbon   Provides an easy method within Word for Windows for changing the appearance of text: for example, adding bold and italics.

rowing   (1) What you want to do if you're in a canoe and you hear a very loud roaring sound. (2) A technique used in moving a mouse with short strokes: move it a little, pick it up (just barely), place it back in the middle of the pad, and move it again.

Ruler   Provides an easy method within Word for Windows for setting tab stops, indentations, and margins.

scaling   The process of resizing a graphic so it does not lose its proportions.

scroll   To move text up/down or right/left on a computer screen.

scroll bars   Located along the bottom and right sides of the Document Window, you use scroll bars to display other areas of the document.

scroll box   Its position within the entire scroll bar tells you roughly where you are within your document.

section   A part of a document that has different settings from the main document for things (such as margins, paper size, headers, footers, columns, and page numbering). A section can be any length: several pages, several paragraphs, or even a single line (such as a heading).

Selection bar   This invisible area that runs along the left side of the document window provides a quick way for you to select a section of text that you want to edit.

selection letters   A single letter of a menu command, such as the *x* in Exit, which activates the command when the menu is open and that letter is pressed.

shading   The box of gray which is placed behind text or a cell in a table in order to emphasize it.

software   Any instructions that tell your computer (the hardware) what to do. There are two types of software: operating system software and application software. *Operating system software* (such as DOS) gets your computer up and running. *Application software* allows you to do something useful, such as type a letter or save the whales.

Spell Checker   A special program within Word for Windows that corrects spelling errors within a document.

Spike   A command within Word for Windows that allows you to copy multiple groups of text to the Clipboard, so they can be placed together within the document with a single command.

split bar   Located on the right-hand side of a document window which, when double-clicked on, will cause that window to split vertically into two windows called *panes*.

spreadsheet   A computer program that organizes information in columns and rows and performs calculations. If you want to balance a checkbook or last year's budget, use a spreadsheet program. Common spreadsheets include Lotus 1-2-3, Microsoft Excel, and Quattro Pro.

Status bar   Located at the bottom of the Program Window, this displays information about your document.

style   A collection of specifications for formatting text. A style may include information for the font, size, style, margins, and spacing. Applying a style to text automatically formats the text according to the style's specifications.

style area   (1) That area in front of the mirrors in every women's restroom. (2) An area that can be made to appear at the far left side of the Word for Windows screen and which displays the style for every paragraph in a document.

tab   (1) A drink that's just one calorie! (2) A keystroke that moves the cursor to a specified point. Used to align columns of text.

table   (1) A great place for my keys and all those bills I haven't paid. (2) Used to organize large amounts of columnar data. Tables consist of rows (the horizontal axis) and columns (the vertical axis). The intersection of a row and a column is called a *cell*.

template   Defines the Word environment, such as margin settings, page orientation, and so on. The template also controls which menu commands are available and what tools appear on the Toolbar. Word for Windows comes with additional templates that you can use to create specialized documents. If you are using one of these templates, your screen may look different than the ones shown in this book. Also, you may have additional commands available on the menus.

text area   The main part of the Document Window; this is where the text you type will appear.

text file   A type of file that contains no special formatting (such as bold), but simply letters, numbers, and such. See also *ASCII file*.

Toolbar   Presents the most common Word commands in an easy to access form. For example, clicking on one of the buttons on the Toolbar saves your document.

trackball   A device that works like an upside-down mouse and requires less desk space for use. Instead of moving the mouse around the desk to move the pointer on-screen, a trackball lets you roll a ball in place to move the pointer. Some arcade video games use devices similar to trackballs.

view mode   A way of looking at a document. Word for Windows comes with several view modes: Normal, Page Layout, and Print Preview.

widow/orphan   A *widow* is the last line of a paragraph that appears alone at the top of the next page. If the first line of the paragraph gets stranded at the bottom of a page, it is called an *orphan*. Just remember that an orphan is left behind.

windows   (1) Something I don't do. (2) A box that is used to display information in part of the screen.

Windows   A nickname that's often used for Microsoft Windows, a graphical interface program (see *GUI*).

Word for Windows   Brought to you by Microsoft. Word for Windows is one of the most popular Windows word processing programs, and the reason you bought this book.

word processor   A program that lets you enter, edit, format, and print text. A word processor is used to type letters, reports, and envelopes, and to complete other tasks you would normally use a typewriter for.

word wrapping   This is a method that word processors use to adjust a paragraph when you insert or delete text so that it fits between the margins. If you add text, everything in the paragraph is moved down. If you delete text, the remaining text is moved up. Even as you're typing text for the first time, when you reach the right-hand margin, you're automatically placed at the beginning of the next line.

This page unintentionally left blank.

Index

E

Installing Word for Windows

Installing Word for Windows is relatively easy—easier than using it actually. In order to install Word for Windows, you don't really need to understand very much at all. If you've used Windows itself (even just a little) you'll be even further ahead of the game. (If you'd like a quick intro to Windows, read Chapter 3 first.) Feel free to ask a PC guru to help you if you feel at all uncomfortable.

1. Turn on your computer. Look for a switch on the front, back, or right-hand side of that big box thing. You may also have to turn on your *monitor* (it looks like a TV but it gets lousy reception).

2. If Windows starts, great! Skip to the next step. If instead you get a rather unassuming DOS prompt that resembles **C>** or **C:\>**, type **WIN** and press **Enter**. Now you should see Windows. If you don't, or if you got an error message (such as **Bad command or file name**), Windows may not be installed, so get a PC guru to help you.

3. Insert the diskette labeled "Setup—Disk 1" into drive A or B.

4. Open the Program Manager's **F**ile menu by clicking on it, and select the **R**un command. If you're using your keyboard, press **Alt** and **F** at the same time, and then press **R**. Congratulations, it's a dialog box!

5. Type either **A:SETUP** or **B:SETUP** in the box that says Command Line:, and then press **Enter**.

6. A screen will appear, asking you to confirm the name of the directory in which the Word program files will be placed. You can change the name of the directory, but most people don't bother. Press **Enter** to continue.

7. You'll see another screen that asks which type of installation you want to use. I'd recommend Complete Installation because it's the easiest. If you don't have enough room, you can choose Minimum Installation, which will install the minimum number of files needed to run Word for Windows. Avoid Custom Installation unless you have help. Click on the appropriate button to continue.

There you go! Follow the instructions you see on-screen; you'll be told when to insert the additional installation disks. If for some reason you want to abandon the installation, you can press **F3**.

More Fun Learning from Alpha Books!

If you enjoyed
The Complete Idiot's Guide to Word for Windows,
then check out these books!

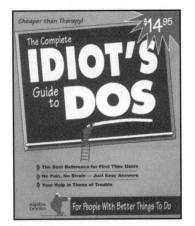

For more information
or to place an order, call

1-800-428-5331

**The Complete Idiot's Guide
to DOS**
ISBN: 1-56761-169-9
Softbound, $14.95 USA

**The Complete Idiot's Guide
to PCs**
ISBN: 1-56761-168-0
Softbound, $14.95 USA

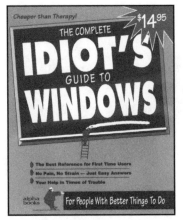

**The Complete Idiot's Guide
to Windows**
ISBN: 1-56761-175-3
Softbound, $14.95 USA